The Christia

Sarah Stancliffe gained a large and enthusiastic following as the cookery writer on the *Church Times*.

She is married to David Stancliffe, the Bishop of Salisbury, and their hospitality is renowned.

The Christian Aid Book of Bread

Recipes to change your world

Sarah Stancliffe

Christian Aid

CANTERBURY
PRESS
Norwich

© Sarah Stancliffe 2005
Cartoons and diagrams Ron Wood 2005
Illustrations Jill Bentley 2005

First published in 2005 by the Canterbury Press Norwich
(a publishing imprint of Hymns Ancient & Modern Limited,
a registered charity)
St Mary's Works, St Mary's Plain,
Norwich, Norfolk, NR3 3BH

www.scm-canterburypress.co.uk

British Library Cataloguing in Publication data

A catalogue record for this book is available
from the British Library

Bible extracts are from the Authorized Version of the Bible
(The King James Bible), the rights in which are vested
in the Crown, are reproduced by permission of the
Crown's Patentee, Cambridge University Press.

ISBN 1-85311-626-2

Typeset by Rowland Phototypesetting Ltd
Bury St Edmunds, Suffolk
Printed and bound by
Bookmarque, Croydon, Surrey

Contents

Contents

Contents

Contents

Acknowledgements

Thanks to Christine Smith of Canterbury Press and Paula Clifford of Christian Aid for the original idea and to Christine for her enthusiastic encouragement.

To Dainis Abolins of Zelta Klingeris bakery in Kuldigas, Latvia, for first showing me rye breadmaking. To Andrew Whitley of the Village Bakery, Melmerby, and Mike Bell of Bells of Lazonby, Cumbria, for their generous encouragement. To the night bakers Philip, Peter and Jim of Nicholas & Harris in Salisbury for their hospitality and answers to all my questions.

Thanks to Anness Publishing Ltd for permission to reproduce the recipe for Christopsomo, Greek Christmas Bread (from *The World Encyclopedia of Bread and Bread-making*, Christine Ingram and Jennie Shapter, Anness Publishing, 2000), and Delia Smith for giving the recipe for Chunky Marmalade Bread and Butter Pudding (from *Delia Smith's Winter Collection*, BBC Worldwide, 1995).

To Jessica and Isobel, who spent a summer half-term afternoon helping to make the Harvest Sheaf.

To David for surviving a bread-based diet for many weeks on end and the others of this household for their honest opinions when tasting.

Above all, to the two brave transcribers of my longhand scrawl on to disk – first Clare Hurst and, more recently, Emma Price, who has borne the brunt of the work with infinite patience and good humour.

Foreword

Bread has been an integral part of family meals and religious celebrations from earliest times, and in its many varied forms it remains a staple food for the world's population. Bread is a vital part of people's diets in rich and poor countries alike, and in some of the world's poorest communities, making bread is an essential activity that enables countless people to earn a living and to provide for their families.

Many of us will probably have enjoyed different types of bread while on holiday or working overseas. Many of us, too, will have resolved to try making them for ourselves once we get home, only to change our minds when confronted with complicated recipes using unfamiliar ingredients. But the compiler of this book, cookery-writer Sarah Stancliffe, fully understands the needs and limitations of even the most hesitant of bread-makers, and helpfully translates into plain English puzzling instructions like 'take a cup of durra'.

The Christian Aid Book of Bread sprang in part from the conviction that harvest suppers, and similar church catering events, should not have to rely on quiches and supermarket loaves. So you will find here tried and tested recipes for all kinds of bread, including festival breads, as well as for dishes based on bread, including some wonderful puddings. But the book also has a deeper purpose: to reflect something of the purpose of Christian Aid itself, in enabling poor communities to feed themselves, while also celebrating the tremendous cultural variety of the countries in which it works.

As this book goes to press, Christian Aid is preparing to celebrate its 60th anniversary. Christian Aid began life after the Second World War as a response of the British and Irish churches to the plight of refugees in Europe. From there it evolved into an organization focusing on disaster relief and longer-term development, with campaigning for the rights of the poor becoming increasingly important. Today it is the official relief and development agency of its many sponsoring churches. In buying this book you are helping Christian Aid's work in more than 50 countries make yet further progress as it embarks on the next 60 years.

Dr Daleep Mukarji
Director, Christian Aid

Introduction

Bread has been a staple food for humankind since we settled down and became farmers rather than hunters. For the poor of the world, famine means having no cereal, having no bread to satisfy their hunger and nourish their bodies. In affluent parts of the world, bread is still important as a staple food and is a major part of our diet in minor meals – breakfast, bread and cheese lunches and teatime, as well as an adjunct to main meals.

For Christians, bread is the ordinary food taken by Christ and made to stand for the supreme sacrifice he made for us, to be re-enacted at each Eucharist, but for non-Christians, too – especially in the Middle East – bread is regarded as a direct gift from God and must not be wasted or thrown away. I hope that this small book will encourage a healthy interest in bread and breadmaking.

> **Wherefore do ye spend money for that which is not bread? and your labour for that which satisfieth not?**
> Isaiah 55.2

There has been a revolution in breadmaking in the past ten years, chiefly because of the invention of breadmaking machines. In the most sophisticated of these, you simply put in the ingredients, adjust the clock, switch it on, go to bed and wake up to a freshly baked loaf. What more could you want?

Introduction

Well, I hope that you will want to experience more – the physical pleasure of mixing and kneading the dough (famously therapeutic), the delight of seeing it rise and the satisfaction of shaping, glazing and baking your own loaves. I think that you will find the taste and texture of handmade bread infinitely better than those of machine-made loaves. You will also be able to make several loaves at a time, and of different shapes.

This book is written for people who want to try making their own bread at home by hand. There are no special skills or complicated equipment required and, apart from the ten minutes or so of kneading in most recipes, very little time of active engagement between each stage. However, most decent bread, with one or two exceptions, does need several hours for the fermentation to happen and the dough to rise. Breadmaking is a perfect activity for anyone at home most of the day, whether minding children or working from home or retired. If you only get home in the evening, you can still make a dough to rise overnight and bake early the next morning, or make a batch of bread at the weekend to last the week.

> The best smell is bread, the best savour is salt, the best love that of children.
>
> George Herbert, *Outlandish Proverbs*

Unlike pastrymaking, bread dough does not require a light touch – indeed, the mixing and kneading need vim and vigour, so anybody can have a go. Children, for instance, love the chance to get their hands into the bowl and learn to pummel the dough until it comes cleanly away from the sides. (Their hands and yours will be softer and cleaner than ever before after mixing and kneading the dough.)

Until I was involved in the research for this book, I had

thought that sourdough bread was not something to attempt at home, but I was quite wrong. Making your own leaven from flour and water could not be simpler – only patience and a warm place are needed – and there is something peculiarly satisfying about making bread with only the simplest ingredients, not even needing bought yeast to make it rise. If you have never tried it, do look at the sourdough recipes in Chapter 1 and have a go.

Before we get started on the recipes, which come from many different countries and cultures, let's look at some simple breadmaking basics.

Basic information

Flour

Buying good flour is no longer a problem, in the West at any rate. Your local supermarket or healthfood shop will stock a wide variety of flours, ground from various grains – wheat, rye, barley, oats, rice, maize and so on.

Wheat flours are the most popular for breadmaking all over the world because wheat grain has a high protein content and it is these proteins that combine to form gluten and give the bread its elasticity and help it to rise.

> I will abundantly bless her provision; I will satisfy her poor with bread.
>
> Psalm 132.15

Other grains, such as rye, barley and maize, are lower in protein and so are often combined with wheat flour to make leavened bread.

Always buy strong, stoneground flours with a high protein content – strong white flour should have 11.5–12g (c. ¼ oz) protein per 100g (4 oz), and strong wholemeal

13–14g (c. ¼–½ oz), which will be marked on the packet. The fresher the flour the better, so buy it where there is a good turnover of stock. Alternatively, find a local miller and buy direct from the mill, in which case you can buy in larger quantities than the usual 1.5kg (3¼lb) bag. Wholemeal flour doesn't keep as long as white, but will be fine for three to four months in a dry, mouse-proof container, such as a small dustbin. Store it in a cool place.

Yeast

Yeast comes in three forms. First, there is fresh compressed baker's yeast, which you can buy from healthfood shops or beg from any supermarket where bread is made on the premises. Store it wrapped in clingfilm in the fridge for 10–12 days or freeze in 25g (½ oz) quantities, using it straight from the freezer as it melts on defrosting. Second, there is dried yeast, which comes in small tins and works perfectly well in most recipes. Finally, Easyblend dried yeast, in sachets – sometimes called Fast Action – is an easier to use form of dried yeast that you mix straight into the flour. For the sake of brevity, I have not given all three options in every recipe, but you can interchange them, except in one or two recipes for rich doughs, such as brioche, where a higher proportion of yeast is used and fresh yeast is best.

There once was a pious young priest
Who lived almost entirely on yeast
For he said, 'It is plain
we must all rise again
And I mean to get started at least.'
Anon

Baking sheets and tins

A couple of large, fairly heavy baking sheets are useful – preferably the kind that are flat with only one end lip, so that you can slide the loaves off easily. Some loaves are shaped and put straight on to the baking sheet, but you will probably want to make loaves in tins, too.

Non-stick, matt loaf tins are best and it is useful to have different sizes – maybe two 0.5-kg (1-lb) and two 1-kg (2-lb) tins. However, you can use any shaped tin that you already have, and some loaves, such as the Italian Panettone, need a round cake tin. Use lard or oil to grease your tins – not butter or margarine, which burn easily. Try not to wash the tins between uses; the loaves should slip out easily and the tins are better left unscrubbed.

The only other equipment you will need is a large mixing bowl, a measuring jug, a rolling pin, occasionally, and a board or smooth surface for kneading and shaping on – and an oven. A nine-muffin tin and a pastry brush may be needed for some recipes.

Storing bread

Always allow loaves to cool thoroughly before storing. Nearly all bread freezes well, so any loaf not to be eaten in the day or two after baking can be wrapped tightly in polythene, labelled and frozen. Allow two to three hours for defrosting, or put the frozen loaf, unwrapped, into a moderate oven for 30 minutes.

For day-to-day bread, a wooden box is the best place to store it. Bread needs some air. Old-fashioned bread crocks had covers pierced with holes. Otherwise damp develops and mould forms. I have a Russian box made of birch bark that is excellent for keeping bread, but any wooden box or drawer would serve. Remove any plastic wrapping before putting the bread into the box.

If the refrigerator is the only cool space you have, then wrap your loaf in thick brown paper or a clean cloth and put it in the salad drawer. Professional bakers wrap loaves in a special wrap that looks like airtight polythene but is in fact peppered with tiny holes.

Remember, too, that the larger the loaf, the longer it will stay fresh. However, bread mould is not necessarily bad for you. In Italy, there is an old custom of eating it to cure chest infections. Maybe we need not worry quite so much if the children nibble it on the way to feed the ducks.

Basic techniques

Although no special skills are required for making bread, it helps to understand the various processes involved.

Mixing, kneading, rising, knocking back and proving

Mixing

Mixing the dry ingredients with the liquids is usually done by making a well in the middle of the flour mixture and gradually adding the liquid, using your hand to mix to make sure that the dry ingredients are evenly and thoroughly wetted. It is easy to leave some dry patches at the bottom of the bowl, so sweep your hand round to incorporate them. This is the stage to add a little more liquid if necessary. Yeast likes warmth rather than high heat, so keep everything warm and do not overheat the liquid. Overheating kills yeast, while underheating just makes it act more slowly.

Kneading

Kneading is an important part of preparing the dough because it helps the gluten to develop and act to lighten the bread.

You should knead on a clean, flat surface, floured to stop the dough sticking. Then, flour your hands, remove the dough from the mixing bowl, place it on your floured surface and press the heel of your hand down into it. Push it away from you and then pull the far edge back over towards you to make a ball shape again. Half turn the ball and press it down again with the heel of your hand and repeat the whole process over and over until the mass of sticky dough miraculously becomes smooth and supple – like an earlobe, as someone put it.

Some doughs are too wet or too rich and soft to knead out of the bowl (such as ciabatta and brioche), but the recipes will guide you as to what to do.

When the dough is smooth and elastic, it is ready to put in a bowl to rise.

Rising

A warm place for rising, such as the back of an Aga, a boiler room or an airing cupboard, is a good way to speed the process along. The dough should be kept airtight at this stage to prevent a skin forming, so oiled clingfilm stretched over the top of the bowl or even a damp cloth covering the top should help.

Depending on the recipe, this first rising may take from one to ten hours. The less yeast used, the slower the rise, but the better the flavour and the keeping qualities of the finished bread.

Knocking back

Knocking back the dough is the next stage. After the dough has risen, you punch it down and deflate it by knocking out the air. Any extra bulky ingredients, such as nuts or fruit, are usually added at this stage, before the final shaping and proving.

Proving

The proving, or final rise, of the loaf is an important stage. If the loaf is underproved, it may rise too fast in the oven, but overproving is worse because the loaf may then collapse. By and large, a loaf needs to rise well, to nearly double in size.

Prove loaves in a warm place, covered with oiled cling-film or a cloth to prevent the top of the dough from drying and crusting.

Slashing, glazing and baking

When the loaf goes into the preheated oven, the gases trapped by the gluten will expand to produce the final 'spring' until the heat kills the yeast.

Slashing

Slashing the top of the unbaked loaf is often recommended to control the 'spring' and make for an even loaf. Use a razor or a very sharp knife. If your loaf is underproved, it will have more spring and so you should slash it deeply. If you have overproved the bread, slash it just a little.

Glazing

Glazing not only gives a handsome finish to the bread, it also provides extra moisture and therefore steam in the oven, which helps the final 'spring' and the setting of the crust. The recipes will guide you on the appropriate glaze.

Baking

Finally, the baking. It is important to preheat your oven for bread. Old-fashioned bakers' ovens began very hot and cooked bread in diminishing heat as the fire burned down. This is why some recipes call for loaves to be baked high up in a hot oven for the first part of the baking and then in a lower heat to finish them.

A wire rack is useful for cooling the finished loaves – they need air all round them.

How to use the recipes

- The ingredients are listed in order of use.
- Quantities are given in metric and imperial measures. Use either metric *or* imperial in each recipe, not a mixture, as the equivalents are not exact.
- Teaspoons is abbreviated as tsp and tablespoons as Tbsp. Use level rather than heaped spoonfuls unless otherwise instructed.
- Oven temperatures are given in centigrade (C), Fahrenheit (F) and gas mark.
- I have given each recipe an estimated 'time to allow'. This is normally from scratch – including assembling and preparing ingredients, time needed for doughs to rise and so on – and so is approximate, as these processes are so variable. However, you will at least be

forewarned about those recipes that take five days from start to finish!

- Eggs are medium unless otherwise specified.

Allergies and special diets

Gluten-free, wheat-free, salt-free and no added fat recipes are marked as such near their titles. Unyeasted recipes are also marked in the text – they include many of the tea-breads and flat breads.

Gluten-free recipes are very few because gluten is so necessary for most bread making. Those on a wheat-free diet might like to try the Russian Rye Bread (page 25). Rye flour has a different gluten from wheat. Bread, especially wholemeal, is high in fibre; you can add extra bran to the Classic Wheat Bread recipes (page 5) – 2–3 tablespoons per 1kg (2lbs 4 oz) of flour – if you want even more fibre.

If you have a child or elderly relative who needs nourishing and likes white bread, use a recipe for dough enriched with eggs and milk (page 9) or add cheese, as in the Welsh Clay Pot Loaf (page 58).

- gluten-free
    Blinis, page 79
    Missi Rotis, page 45
    Oatcakes, page 56

- wheat-free
    Blinis, page 79
    Missi Rotis, page 45
    Oatcakes, page 56
    Russian Rye Bread, page 25

- salt-free
  Pane Basso, page 71
  Sudanese Kisera, page 31

- no added fat
  Baguettes, page 61
  Baltic Sourdough Bread, page 23
  English Cottage Loaf, page 49
  Grant Loaf, page 3
  Pain de Campagne, page 15
  Pan de Cebada, page 17
  Prosphora, page 123
  Russian Rye Bread, page 25
  San Francisco Sourdough, page 20
  Sudanese Kisera, page 31

1

Basic breads and sourdoughs

This first chapter provides some basic recipes for everyday bread, including some variations on the theme. In its second part, it describes how to make sourdough 'starters' and sourdough breads, which have been so important in the history of breadmaking.

THE GRANT LOAF

No added fat
Allow 1½–2 hours

Doris Grant's recipe for wholemeal bread was first published in 1944, when British households were still in the grip of wartime rations and privations. Her fatless loaf is so simple and so quick to make that it is an ideal way in to making your own bread. Only one rise, in the tin, is involved and the whole process, from start to finish, should not take more than one and a half hours.

Doris Grant was an early campaigner for healthy eating and an evangelist for the health-giving properties of wholemeal bread, but you can in fact make this loaf with strong white flour, malted Granary flour or a mixture of flours. These lighter loaves make wonderful toast three or four days later.

Makes 2 large or 3 medium loaves

> 1.4kg/3lbs stoneground wholemeal flour
> 15g/3 tsp salt
> 1 Tbsp Easyblend dried yeast
> 1 Tbsp muscovado sugar
> 1.2 litres/2 pints warm water

For quickest results, warm the mixing bowl with the flour first. Grease 2 large tins or 3 medium ones with lard or oil (butter or margarine tends to burn).

Mix the flour, salt, yeast and sugar in a large bowl. Make a well in the middle and pour in the water. Mix thoroughly by hand until the dough comes away from the sides of the bowl. It will still be wet enough to stick to your fingers. Divide the dough between the tins, scraping your fingers clean with a spoon handle, cover with a clean cloth and put in a warm place to rise for about 30 minutes, until the dough has risen to within 1cm/½in of the rim.

Preheat the oven to 200°C/400°F/gas mark 6.

Bake in the preheated oven for 40–50 minutes. The top should be crusty and the loaf sound hollow when you turn it out on to a rack to cool. There is no need to wash the tins before the next baking, as long as the loaves have turned out cleanly.

CLASSIC WHEAT BREAD
(brown or white)

Know ye not that a little leaven leaveneth the whole
lump?

1 Corinthians 5.6

Allow 2½–3½ hours

Makes 2 medium loaves or 24 rolls

900g/2lbs stoneground wholemeal or strong white flour
   or a mixture
10g/2 tsp salt
15g/½ oz fresh yeast or 2 tsp Easyblend dried yeast
600ml/c. 1 pint warm water
60ml/2fl oz vegetable oil

Heat your oven to its minimum temperature or use the
lowest Aga oven. Put the flour and salt into a mixing bowl
and warm through in the oven for 5–10 minutes.

Make a well in the middle of the flour mixture, crumble
the fresh yeast into it and pour in a third of the water,
stirring with your fingers. Leave for 5 minutes, then add
the rest of the water and the oil. (If using Easyblend dried
yeast, simply mix it in with the flour and add the water all
at once.)

Mix all together thoroughly by hand until the dough
comes cleanly away from the sides of the bowl. Turn it out
on to a floured surface and knead for 5–10 minutes until it
is smooth and elastic. Return it to the bowl, cover with
oiled clingfilm and leave in a warm place to rise until it has
doubled in size – probably 1–1½ hours.

Turn it out again on to the floured surface and knock
it back. Divide the dough into 2 balls. Grease 2 medium

5

(1-kg/2-lb) loaf tins and lay a ball in each, shaping it into an oblong to fit the tin. Cover again with oiled clingfilm or a damp cloth and leave to prove in a warm place until they rise to within 1cm/½in of the top of the tins.

Meanwhile, raise the oven temperature to 230°C/450°F/gas mark 8.

Bake for 30–35 minutes on a middle shelf. Turn one out to see if it sounds hollow when tapped on the bottom. If you want them crisper, return to the oven for another 10 minutes without the tins.

Cool on a rack.

You can use the same dough to make rolls instead of loaves. Just divide the dough into 24 equal pieces, shape them after the rising and knocking back, put them on a floured baking sheet to prove and bake for about 15 minutes in a 220°C/425°F/gas mark 7 oven. Different-shaped rolls are fun – see the recipe Enriched dough for white bread and rolls, page 9, for shapes.

SAVOURY BREADS

Allow 3–4 hours

These are variations on the Classic Wheat Bread recipe (page 5), adding olives or onions or sunflower seeds before the first proving. If you want to make two different loaves at the same time, make all the dough, divide it before the first rising and add half the quantity of your chosen flavouring to each.

Makes 2 loaves

  450g/1lb strong white flour
  1½ tsp salt
  2 tsp Easyblend dried yeast or 15g/½ oz fresh yeast
  450ml/¾ pint warm water
  2 Tbsp olive oil
  12–15 large black olives, stoned and halved, or 2 medium onions, sliced and softened in olive oil, or 75g/2 oz sunflower seeds, lightly toasted under the grill or in a dry frying pan.

Mix the flour, salt and Easyblend dried yeast in a large, warm bowl. (If using fresh yeast, crumble it into a well in the middle of the flour mixture.) Add the warm water and olive oil gradually, mixing by hand until it comes together as a dough. Now add your extra ingredient – the olives, onions or toasted sunflower seeds (see the note above about making two different loaves) and turn it all out on to a floured surface.

Knead for 5 minutes or so, until it is smooth and elastic and no longer sticky. Return the dough to the bowl, cover with oiled clingfilm and set aside in a warm place to double in size – 1–2 hours.

Turn the dough out again on to the floured surface, knock down and divide it into two. Shape each half into an oval and lay them on a greased baking sheet, side by side, not too close. Cover with oiled clingfilm and leave again to prove for 30–40 minutes.

Preheat the oven to 220°C/425°F/gas mark 7. Slash the tops of the loaves diagonally and bake for 30–40 minutes, until golden brown. They should sound hollow when tapped on the bottom. Cool on a wire rack.

If they last long enough to become slightly stale, all these breads are delicious toasted. The olive and onion versions are, of course, best with savoury food, while the sunflower seed bread is just as good with cheese or honey.

ENRICHED DOUGH FOR WHITE BREAD AND ROLLS

Allow 2½–3½ hours

Makes 3 medium loaves or 24 rolls or 1 loaf and 16 rolls

> 900g/2lbs strong white flour
> 10g/2 tsp caster sugar
> 30g/1 oz fresh yeast
> 600ml/c. 1 pint warm milk or milk and water
> 10g/2 tsp salt
> 120g/4 oz butter
> 2 eggs

Glaze and decoration

> 1 egg yolk
> 1 Tbsp water
> poppy and sesame seeds

Knot

Trefoil

Plait

Cottage roll

Mix 100g/4 oz of the flour, the sugar, yeast (crumbled), and all the milk or milk and water in a large mixing bowl. Set in a warm place for about 20 minutes, until it looks bubbly and alive.

Mix the remaining flour with the salt and rub in the butter. Beat the eggs and add to the yeast mixture with the dry ingredients. Mix well to a soft dough, adding a little more flour if it is too sticky to handle.

Turn the dough out on to a floured surface and knead for 5–10 minutes until smooth and elastic. Return the dough to the large bowl and cover with oiled clingfilm. Leave in a warm place to rise until doubled in size.

Turn the dough out on to the floured surface again, knock back and knead for a minute or two. Take small pieces (50g/2 oz each) and shape as you like. Here are some ideas.

- Plaits

    Make 3 thin strands, join together at one end, plait evenly, from the sides inwards, pinch the ends together to join and tuck under.

- Knots

    Make 1 long snake and tie it into a single knot, leaving the ends sticking out.

- Trefoils

    Make 3 small balls from the piece of dough and place together in triangular formation, sides touching each other.

- Mini cottage rolls

    Take two thirds of a piece, shape it into a ball, set the other third in a ball on top, press a hole through the middle with your finger.

Place your shaped rolls on greased baking sheets, well spaced, and cover with oiled clingfilm to prove until doubled in size – 20–30 minutes.

Preheat the oven to 200°C/425°F/gas mark 7.

To make the glaze, mix the egg yolk and water and brush over the rolls. Sprinkle some with poppy, some with sesame, seeds. Bake in the preheated oven for 15–18 minutes, or until golden. Lift on to a wire rack to cool.

For loaves, either put them in greased tins to prove or shape into a cob or cottage loaf, place on a greased baking sheet and glaze as the rolls.

SWEET BREAD DOUGH

Add 75g (3 oz) caster sugar in the second step with the rest of the flour before adding the yeast mixture. This makes a good basis for all sorts of buns and teabreads.

SOURDOUGH BREADS

Making sourdough takes us back to the earliest origin of yeasted breadmaking. We think that about two millennia ago, the Egyptians – expert flatbread makers – discovered the effect of natural yeasts by accident, leaving a piece of dough out for some hours so that the flour and water had time to ferment before being baked.

Such a wonderful discovery soon spread throughout the rest of the civilised world and, although today we mostly use bakers' yeast, the sourdough tradition continues in much of Europe. There is something peculiarly satisfying about making a loaf from start to finish with nothing but flour, water and salt.

Some sourdough breads use just a natural leaven, which is made by leaving flour and water to ferment spontaneously over 2–3 days. It develops a lovely appley, slightly sour smell and you then continue the recipe by adding more flour and water according to instructions.

Other sourdoughs, notably Italian ones, use a yeasted

BREAD WAS INVENTED ACCIDENTALLY
WHEN RAMESES THE CARELESS LEFT THE
CHEESE OUT OF A CHEESE ROLL

starter, including a small piece of fresh bakers' yeast. Here are the recipes for each sort of starter.

NATURAL LEAVEN STARTER
(called a 'chef' in France)

Allow 3–4 days

> 3 Tbsp warm water
> 60g/2 oz wholemeal flour

Add the water to the flour in a small bowl and mix with your fingers until it makes a firm dough. Cover with a cloth and leave in a warm place for 2–3 days. It will form a crust, but the inside will be moist and smell sweet. Pull off the crust, discard and put the moist centre into a larger bowl for the 1st refreshment (see below).

1st refreshment

> 4 Tbsp warm water
> 120g/4 oz wholemeal flour

Add the water to the natural leaven starter in the bowl and mix well with your fingers. Add the flour to make a dough and knead for 3–4 minutes. Cover with oiled clingfilm and leave again in a warm place for 1 more day. The smell will be more lively now. Discard the crust again for the 2nd refreshment (see below).

2nd refreshment

120ml/4fl oz warm water
180g/6 oz strong white flour

Mix as for 1st refreshment above, then leave the dough covered with oiled clingfilm in the warm place for about 10 hours, when it should have doubled in size. Your sourdough starter is now ready to use.

YEASTED STARTER
('biga' in Italian)

Allow 12–15 hours

175g/6 oz strong white flour
7g/¼ oz fresh yeast
6 Tbsp warm water

Make a well in the middle of the flour, crumble in the yeast and mix in the water with your fingers, gradually bringing in all the flour to make a firm dough. Knead for a little until smooth, then leave in a bowl covered with oiled clingfilm in a warm place overnight (12–15 hours). It should rise and then fall back and is then ready to use.

PAIN DE CAMPAGNE
(FRENCH COUNTRY BREAD)

No added fat
Allow 3–4 days for the 'chef'
Allow 4–5 hours for the loaf

Makes 1 large loaf

'chef' natural leaven starter (see page 13)
220ml/8fl oz warm water
450g/1lb strong white flour or white and brown mixed
2 tsp salt

Place the 'chef' starter in a large bowl, mix the water into it with your fingers, then gradually add the flour and salt. Turn the dough out on to a floured surface and knead for 5–10 minutes, until smooth and elastic. Return the dough to the bowl, cover with oiled clingfilm and put it in a warm place to rise until it has almost doubled in size – 1½–3 hours.

Turn the dough out again on to your floured surface, knock back and take off a small piece (c. 100g/4 oz) to start the next loaf. Store this in a small bowl, covered with clingfilm, in the fridge.

Shape the remaining dough into a ball. Line a round basket or bowl (23–25cm/9–10in diameter, 1–2 litre/2 pint capacity) with a floured cloth and place the dough inside, seam side up. Cover again with oiled clingfilm and put in a warm place to rise until it has nearly doubled in size – about 1 hour.

Preheat the oven to 230°C/450°F/gas mark 8 and oil a baking sheet.

Turn the risen loaf out on to the prepared baking sheet and slash the top with a sharp knife, making 4 cuts at right angles to each other, as if for noughts and crosses, for the traditional pattern.

Bake for 25–30 minutes, until nicely browned and it sounds hollow when tapped on the bottom.

Cool on a wire rack.

Use the reserved piece of sourdough to save time when you are next baking – start then at the 2nd refreshment.

PAN DE CEBADA (SPANISH BARLEY BREAD)

No added fat
Allow 2 days

This country bread uses a sourdough starter, which gives it a wonderful depth of flavour. Barley and maize flours are low in gluten and so need wheat flour to help them rise. You need to start this loaf two days before you want to eat it.

Makes 1 large loaf

Sourdough starter

> 175g/6 oz maize meal
> 560ml/1 pint water
> 225g/8 oz strong wholemeal flour
> 75g/3 oz barley flour

In a small saucepan, mix the maize meal with half the water and gradually stir in the rest of the water. Cook gently, stirring all the time until it thickens. Spoon it out into a large bowl and allow to cool.

Mix in the wholemeal and barley flours to make a soft dough. Turn it out on to a floured surface and knead for about 5 minutes. Return the dough to the bowl, cover with a damp cloth and leave in a warm place for about 36 hours. It will ferment, rise and smell appley.

Dough

> 20g/¾ oz fresh yeast or 1 Tbsp Easyblend dried yeast
> 3 Tbsp warm water
> 225g/8 oz strong wholemeal flour

1 Tbsp salt
maize meal, for dusting

If using fresh yeast, cream it in a small bowl with the warm water. Stir this mixture into the sourdough starter with the wholemeal flour and salt (add the Easyblend dried yeast now, if using instead) and work to a dough. Turn it out on to a floured surface and knead for a few minutes, until smooth and elastic. Return it to the large bowl, cover with oiled clingfilm and leave it in a warm place to double in size – 1–2 hours.

Scatter maize meal thickly over a baking sheet. Knock back the dough and shape it into a ball. Place it on the baking sheet and sprinkle with a little maize meal. Cover with a large upturned bowl and leave to prove until it has almost doubled in size – about 1 hour.

When the dough has risen, preheat the oven to 220°C/ 425°F/gas mark 7 and place an empty roasting tin in the bottom of the oven. Pour 300ml/½ pint cold water into the tin. Remove the bowl and put the baking sheet and loaf in the oven above the steaming tin of water.

Bake for 10 minutes, then remove the tin of water and reduce the heat to 190°C/375°F/gas mark 5 (in an Aga, simply put in the cold shelf) and bake for another 20–25 minutes, until deep golden and hollow-sounding when tapped on the bottom.

Cool on a wire rack.

PANE PUGLIESE (ITALIAN COUNTRY BREAD)

... oil to make his face shine, and bread which strengtheneth man's heart.

Psalm 104.15

Allow 12 hours for the 'biga'
Allow 4–5 hours for the loaf

Makes 1 large loaf

'biga' yeasted starter (see page 14)
275ml/9fl oz warm water
15g/½ oz fresh yeast
2 tsp salt
2 tsp olive oil
225g/8 oz strong white flour
225g/8 oz stoneground wholemeal flour

Place the 'biga' in a large mixing bowl and mix the warm water into it. Crumble in the yeast, add the salt and use your fingers to dissolve the 'biga'. Add the olive oil and then the flours, gradually, beating with your hand all the time.

Mix to a dough and knead on a floured surface for about 10 minutes, until smooth and elastic. Return the dough to the bowl, cover with oiled clingfilm and put it in a warm place to prove until it has at least doubled in volume – about 2 hours.

Oil and warm a baking sheet. Knock back and shape the dough into a ball. Turn it out on to the prepared baking sheet, cover again with oiled clingfilm and leave to rise for another 1–1½ hours.

Preheat the oven to 230°C/450°F/gas mark 8, then bake the loaf for 30–35 minutes, until it sounds hollow when tapped on the bottom. Cool on a wire rack.

SAN FRANCISCO SOURDOUGH

No added fat

If you have some sourdough starter ready (see page 17), begin at Step 2. Otherwise use a walnut-sized piece of dough reserved from any previous baking.

Step 1

Allow 6–9 hours for the leaven

> 60ml/2fl oz cold water
> walnut-sized piece of dough reserved from previous
>   baking
> 120g/4 oz stoneground wholemeal flour
> pinch cumin

Mix the water and the dough, then add the flour and cumin, mixing them together with your fingertips to make a firm but moist dough. You may need a little more water to achieve this consistency. Put the dough in a small bowl, cover with oiled clingfilm and leave in a warm place to double in size – 6–9 hours.

Step 2

Allow 8–12 hours

> leaven made in Step 1
> 350ml/12fl oz warm water
> 15g/½ oz fresh yeast
> 425g/15 oz strong white flour

Mix the leaven with the water and yeast in a large bowl to make a 'soup'.

Add the flour gradually, beating well with your hand for at least 10 minutes to make the gluten as elastic as possible. Cover the bowl with oiled clingfilm and leave in a warm place for 8–12 hours. It will look bubbly and smell sweetly sour.

Step 3

Allow 2½ hours

> 300g/10 oz strong white flour
> 2 tsp salt
> ½ tsp bicarbonate of soda

Mix the flour, salt and bicarbonate of soda, then add to the bubbly mixture in the bowl. Mix to a dough, then turn it out on to a floured surface and knead well for 15–20 minutes, until smooth and springy.

Divide the dough into 2 balls, placing each on a greased baking sheet. Cover them with oiled clingfilm and leave to rise in a warm place for 1½ hours. They will spread.

Preheat the oven to 230°C/450°F/gas mark 8. Slash the tops of the loaves, forming a criss-cross pattern, dust with a little flour and bake for 25 minutes – if possible, spraying the oven with water once or twice to make steam. Another way to make steam is to put an empty roasting tin in the bottom of a hot oven, then, when you put in the bread, drop several ice cubes into the hot pan and close the door. The crust will be delicious.

Cool on wire racks.

SOURDOUGH RYE BREADS

Sourdough has a particular affinity with rye – the flavours seem to complement each other. My first experience of watching rye bread being made was in Latvia, where the profits from the traditional bakery had helped finance the building of a new local church. They still used the old oak tubs to ferment the sourdough leaven, never washing them out so that the next batch uses the yeasts in the old leaven to start it off again.

The Latvians shaped their rye bread with wet hands – rye dough is very sticky – and the finished loaves were large, weighing in at 3kg (7lbs) each. The whole process took 32 hours from start to finish. Loaves that are a long time in the making keep well; the shop shelflife of those Latvian loaves was ten days. Ours lasted two weeks in good condition.

Rye has some gluten, but it is different from wheat gluten, so some people who are allergic to wheat are able to eat rye bread – as long as wheat flour is not added, of course, though rye alone makes a dense loaf. See the recipe for Russian Rye Bread (page 25) if you want to make a wheat-free loaf. Here first, though, is a recipe for a more common Baltic Sourdough bread, which uses rye and wheat flours. It is based on an old Latvian recipe and uses both a sourdough starter and ordinary yeast.

BALTIC SOURDOUGH BREAD

No added fat
Allow 2–3 days for the starter
Allow 8–12 hours for 2nd stage, 2½–3 hours for the loaf

Makes 1 large or 2 medium loaves

300g/10 oz rye flour
300ml/10fl oz warm water
60g/2 oz sourdough starter (see Natural leaven starter,
    page 13, preferably made with rye or wheat flour)
120g/4 oz molasses
30g/1 oz fresh yeast or 2 tsp Easyblend dried yeast
660g/1lb 6 oz strong white flour
2 tsp salt
4 tsp caraway seeds
more warm water, to mix

Put the rye flour in a large bowl. Add a little of the warm water to the sourdough starter in another small bowl to slacken it, then stir this into the rye flour, adding the rest of the water gradually to make a wet dough. Cover the bowl with a cloth and leave in a warm place overnight or for at least 8 hours. It should smell and taste like sour apples.

The next day, stir in the molasses, the yeast and then the white flour, salt and caraway seeds and mix to a manageable dough, using more warm water as necessary.

Turn the dough out on to a floured surface and knead it well until it loses its stickiness. Return it to the bowl, cover it this time with oiled clingfilm and leave in the warm to double in size – about 1½ hours.

Turn the dough out on to a floured surface, knock back and, wetting your hands, shape it into 1 large or 2 medium loaves that are oval rather than round. Place the loaf or loaves on a greased baking sheet, cover again and leave in a warm place to prove for 30 minutes. Preheat the oven to 200°C/400°F/gas mark 6.

Now slash the dough diagonally 3 or 4 times, wet the surface again and bake in the centre of the preheated oven, allowing 40–60 minutes for a large loaf or 35–40 minutes for the medium loaves, until they sound hollow when tapped on the bottom.

Cool on a wire rack.

RUSSIAN RYE BREAD

Wheat-free
No added fat
Overall time from start to eating: 4½ days

This bread – which uses only rye flour, natural leaven, no added fat and is low in salt – takes a long time to make but keeps well and has a wonderful flavour. It is similar to the Rossisky bread, marketed by the Village Bakery in Melmerby, Cumbria, and I am grateful to the night bakers at Nicholas & Harris in Salisbury for their help in adapting the recipe for home baking.

Quite deep tins – 9–10cm (3½–4in) deep – are needed for this recipe. If you don't have two deep, rectangular tins, you could use deep round cake tins. I use one rectangular tin that is 18 x 13 x 10cm (7 x 5 x 4in) and one round tin 9cm deep and 18cm across (3½ by 7in). I line the bottom of the round tin with non-stick baking parchment as it is not normally used for bread and may stick.

You may prefer to make just one loaf first time round, halving the quantities, but these large, dense loaves do keep well and will freeze.

Makes 2 large loaves (see above for tins)

Starter

Allow 2 days

> 60g/2 oz stoneground rye flour
> 60ml/2fl oz warm water

Mix together to form a dough in a small bowl. Cover with a cloth and leave in a warm place for 2 days to ripen, stirring twice a day to prevent crusting.

Leaven

Allow 8–10 hours or overnight

300g/10 oz stoneground rye flour
the starter (see above)
300ml/10fl oz warm water

Put the flour into a large bowl, make a well in the middle
and put the starter in it. Gradually add the water to
slacken the starter as you mix, mixing in the rest of the
flour as you go. Beat it well – it should be quite soft and
damp – then cover with a damp cloth and leave it in a
warm place to develop overnight.

Dough

Allow 3 hours and then 2 days before eating

660g/1lb 6 oz stoneground rye flour
20g/¾ oz sea salt
570ml/1 pint, or more, warm water

The next morning, when the leaven smells beautifully
sour, grease your 2 loaf tins (see above). Beat in the flour
and salt gradually, aiming at a soft dough. Add as much
water as you need to achieve this consistency. Use your
hand, but it will be very sticky, so have a bowl of water
nearby to wet it frequently.

Knead the mixture in the bowl until it comes away from
the sides and is smooth and slippery. Place half the dough
in each greased tin, wet your hand and flatten the surface.
The tins, whichever size you choose, should be only half
full of dough. Cover them with oiled clingfilm and put to
prove in a warm place for about 1 hour.

Shortly before the dough is ready, preheat the oven to 220°C/425°F/gas mark 7.

When the dough has begun to rise in the tins, but before it reaches the top, wet the tops again. Set them in the centre of the preheated oven and bake for 50–60 minutes altogether – the first 30 minutes at the high heat, then reduce to 190°C/375°F/gas mark 5 for the final 30 minutes. Test to see if they sound hollow when tapped and don't be afraid to cook them longer if in doubt.

Cool thoroughly on a rack before storing.

Best eaten after 2 days, in thin slices.

NB: The Rossisky bread uses light and dark rye flour, in the proportion 2:1, which gives more depth of flavour. Most supermarkets and healthfood shops only sell light rye flour, though, so I have used that.

2

Breads from around the world

This chapter shows the amazing variety of breads that are made around the world, from African flatbreads, through the Welsh Clay Pot Loaf to Italian ciabatta and Russian blinis.

Some of the breads can only be an approximation to the native originals because of differences in ingredients (French and American flours are both different from English flour, for instance) or cooking apparatus (most of us can muster neither a steam oven nor a charcoal fire). Making the various breads helps us to identify with the

people whose daily fare we are replicating, however inadequately. For those of us living a comfortable Western life where food is easily available, to make Sudanese Kisera and remember that many Sudanese eat only every other day is a small act of solidarity.

Africa

KISERA (SUDANESE PANBREAD)

> And they shall eat the flesh in that night, roast with fire,
> and unleavened bread; and with bitter herbs they shall
> eat it.
>
> Exodus 12.8

Salt-free
Unyeasted
Allow 2 days

In the Sudan, the women often spend much of the morning crouching over a charcoal fire, cooking their sourdough pancakes on a huge flat iron griddle. As they are
made, looking like rather grey cloths, they are folded
in four and kept in a great pile, ready for the meal of the
day. Guests, having washed their hands in the bowl of
water brought to them, take a kisera and tear off pieces to
use instead of implements as a scoop for the spicy stew
provided.

In the Sudan, the flour used is 'durra', from sorghum or
Indian millet – a grain grown in arid countries that is full
of minerals, but lacks the gluten needed for leavened
bread. Here we can only make an approximation with
wheat flour. It has no salt, but the sour starter gives it
some flavour.

There are no scales in Africa, so I give the recipe as it
came to me from the women of the Diocese of Renk, with
a few adjustments along the way. My 'cup' holds 115g/
4 oz flour.

Take 1 cup of durra or wheat flour and mix it with half
a cup of warm water. Leave to ferment in a warm place

for 24 hours or so. It should form a crust and smell like yeast. Alternatively, use 2 tablespoons sourdough starter if you have some already (see page 17).

Peel the crust off the sourdough starter and stir in 1½ more cups of warm water, beating in 3 cups of flour (use a mixture of plain white and wholemeal) as you go, making a batter that is thicker than usual for pancakes, but slacker than a bread dough. Add more water if need be. Cover with a damp cloth and leave in a warm place for 12–24 hours to ferment again. The longer you leave it, the more pleasantly sour the flavour.

Warm a griddle with a very little oil. Take a large spoonful (or a small cup) of the batter and pour it on to the griddle, spreading it quickly with the back of the spoon (the women in the Sudan use a palm leaf) to cover the pan as thinly as possible. I find pouring it in a wide circle and spreading it inwards works better than trying to spread it from a pool in the middle outwards.

Cook for 2–3 minutes, until the batter has dried through and the edges are lifting. Do not turn. Peel it off the griddle (a fish slice is useful, though unauthentic) and stack on a clean teacloth. Fold them in four for serving. Continue until the batter is finished. This amount makes about 12 medium-sized pancakes.

You may need to re-oil the griddle occasionally. In the Sudan they use 'thiuk' (from an animal's brain) for this but I have not searched for that here.

Americas

NEW ENGLAND FANTANS

Allow 2½–3 hours

These fantail rolls are crisp and light – perfect with soup at a dinner party or for children to enjoy, pulling off the sections one by one. You need a muffin tin with nine 7.5-cm (3-in) cups.

Makes 9

> 15g/½ oz fresh yeast or 1 Tbsp Easyblend dried yeast
> 75ml/5 Tbsp buttermilk or yogurt and milk mixed
> 2 tsp caster sugar
> 75ml/5 Tbsp milk
> 65g/2½ oz butter
> 375g/13 oz strong white flour
> 1 tsp salt
> 1 egg, lightly beaten

Grease the muffin tin.
 Mix the fresh yeast with the buttermilk or yoghurt and milk mixture and sugar and leave in a warm place for 15 minutes.

New England Fantans

Heat the milk with 40g (1½ oz) of the butter (reserve the remainder) until it has melted. Cool to lukewarm. Sift the flour and salt into a large bowl – add the Easyblend dried yeast at this point, if using. Add the yeast mixture, milk and butter mixture and the egg to the bowl and mix to form a soft dough.

Turn out on to a floured surface and knead for 5–8 minutes, until smooth and elastic. Put the dough back in the large bowl, cover with oiled clingfilm and leave in a warm place for about 1 hour, until doubled in size.

Turn out again, knock back and knead for a few minutes. Roll into a rectangle about 45 by 30cm (18 by 12in), about 5mm (¼in) thick. Melt the remaining butter and brush it all over the dough.

Cut the dough lengthways into 5 equal strips. Stack them on top of each other, reversing the last strip, so that butter meets butter, then cut the stack across into 9 equal pieces, each 5cm (2in) square. For each, pinch one side of the stacked squares together and place it pinched side down into a cup in the prepared muffin tin. Cover with the oiled clingfilm and leave to double in size – probably 30–40 minutes.

Meanwhile, preheat the oven to 200°C/400°F/gas mark 6. Bake for 20 minutes, or until golden.

Turn out and cool on a wire rack.

BOSTON BROWN BREAD

Unyeasted
Allow 2–2½ hours

The cylindrical shape of this dark, rich bread makes it very attractive and easy to serve. It betrays its New England settler origins by being steamed, rather than baked, by the container used to make it in, and by the mixture of grains used. If you have only two of the three grains listed for the recipe, simply increase the quantity of each to make 250g (9 oz) altogether.

You will need a 1.2-litre (2-pint) cylindrical tin or heat-proof glass container. The glass jug from a 1.2-litre (2-pint) filter coffee maker is ideal, but will be less authentic than an empty tin, or two 450-g (1-lb) tins. Whatever you use will need to fit inside a deep saucepan. If you are lucky enough to have a tall asparagus pan, it holds the jug or tin perfectly.

Makes 1 large loaf or 2 small (see above)

   90g/3 oz wholemeal flour
   90g/3 oz rye flour
   90g/3 oz cornmeal
   ½ tsp salt
   1 tsp bicarbonate of soda
   230ml/8fl oz milk and water, mixed half and half
   90ml/3fl oz black treacle or molasses

Grease the glass jug or tin container(s) well and line the base with a disc of greaseproof paper.

Mix the flours, salt and bicarbonate of soda together in a large bowl. Warm the milk and water mixture in a saucepan and stir in the treacle or molasses. Add this to the bowl and stir together just enough to make a moist dough.

Spoon the mixture into the prepared container(s) (to about two-thirds full) and cover with foil or greaseproof paper, tied on securely.

Put a trivet (or an upturned enamel plate) in the bottom of a deep pan, stand the glass jug or tin container on it and half fill the pan with boiling water. Cover the pan and steam for 1½–2 hours, adding more boiling water now and then if needed. If using 2 tins, cook one and then the other.

Remove the jug or tin from the water, leave to stand for a few minutes, then turn out on to a wire rack.

Best eaten fresh and warm, this bread is delicious with cheese or baked beans.

CORN BREAD

Unyeasted
Allow 45 minutes

As Christopher Columbus found when he reached the Americas, wheat was unknown and the staple crop was maize (corn). This had been developed from a wild Mexican grass some 5000 years earlier. To the ancient Aztecs, maize was the focus of their religion – the greatest corn god being called Quetzalcoatl, with a sprouting maize cob as his emblem. Maize spread from Mexico across Central America and then North America and South America, where the Incas developed a type with larger, starchy kernels.

Today, there are many types and colours of corn – yellow, white, purple, blue, red and black. In Britain, however, we can only usually find yellow cornmeal in the shops, so here is a recipe using that and incorporating tinned sweetcorn, too.

Makes 1 medium bread

75g/3 oz strong white flour
150g/6 oz yellow cornmeal
1 tsp salt
1½ Tbsp baking powder
1 Tbsp caster sugar
50g/2 oz butter, melted
250ml/8fl oz milk
3 eggs
200g/7 oz tinned sweetcorn, drained

Preheat the oven to 200°C/400°F/gas mark 6. Grease and line the base of a 22-cm (8½-in) round or square cake tin.

Sift the flour, cornmeal, salt and baking powder into a large bowl. Stir in the sugar and make a well in the middle.

Mix the melted butter, milk and eggs together. Pour into the well you have made in the flour and stir briskly until just mixed. Stir in the drained sweetcorn, then pour the mixture into the prepared tin.

Bake in the preheated oven for 20–25 minutes. Test by inserting a skewer into the middle of the Corn Bread – it will come out clean when it is done. Invert the cooked bread on to a wire rack and remove the lining paper.

Serve warm, cut in wedges. Delicious with fried bacon or baked ham instead of potatoes.

MEXICAN TORTILLAS

Unyeasted
Allow 1 hour

The Aztecs and Maya peoples of Mexico made tortillas from dry maize kernels by soaking and boiling the corn in lime water and then grinding it to a paste. From this paste – called 'nixtamal' – fresh masa is derived, from which true tortillas are made. However, here we can only buy masa harina – maize flour – which makes the tortillas much more difficult to fashion, even if you have a tortilla press. I think a better solution – which is also authentic, at least for northern Mexico and the south west states of America – is to make wheat tortillas.

Makes 12

> 300g/10 oz unbleached plain white flour (not strong)
> 1 tsp salt
> 1 tsp baking powder
> 50g/2 oz lard
> c. 175ml/6fl oz hot water

Mix the flour, salt and baking powder together in a bowl. Rub in the lard with your fingertips, stir in the hot water and mix to a soft dough. It will be quite soft, but should not turn into a batter. Cover with clingfilm and leave to rest for 15–20 minutes.

Divide the dough into 12 pieces and shape them into balls. You will need to flour your hands well and reflour the surface as you roll each ball of dough out into a round 15–18cm (6–7in) across. Keep the finished tortillas covered with a cloth to stop them drying out. Heat a griddle or heavy bottomed frying pan, without greasing, and cook one tortilla at a time, turning as soon as the surface bubbles. They need only a minute or less each side so that they remain soft. Stack them in a teacloth while you cook the others. Eat them warm or reheat wrapped in foil in a moderate oven for 4 minutes.

Asia

NAN BREAD

Allow 2–2½ hours

Nan breads are traditionally baked in a 'tandoor', which is a clay oven used in India, and are served with kebabs, though they are delicious accompanying any spicy food. They are like a richer version of the Middle Eastern pitta breads.

Makes 8

- 15g/½ oz fresh yeast or 1 Tbsp Easyblend dried yeast
- 4 Tbsp warm water
- 1 tsp sugar
- 500g/1lb strong white flour or half strong, half normal strength
- 1 tsp salt
- 150ml/¼ pint milk
- 150-g/5-oz carton natural yogurt
- 1 egg, beaten
- 25g/1 oz butter, melted

Glaze

- 1 egg yolk, beaten
- 1 tsp poppy or onion seeds

If using fresh yeast, stir it into the warm water in a small bowl together with the sugar and leave to dissolve and froth – about 10 minutes.

Sift the flour and salt into a large bowl – adding the Easyblend dried yeast now, if using.

Heat the milk until lukewarm. Remove the pan from the heat, then add the yogurt, fresh yeast mixture, beaten egg and melted butter.

Make a well in the middle of the flour and gradually pour in the milk and yogurt mixture, stirring it in with your hand to make a soft dough. Knead it either in the bowl or on a clean, floured surface for 5–10 minutes until it is smooth and elastic, adding a little more flour if need be. Return the dough to the bowl, cover with oiled cling-film and leave in a warm place to double in bulk – 1–1½ hours.

Preheat the oven to 230°C/450°F/gas mark 8 and heat 2 ungreased baking sheets in it.

Divide the dough into 8 pieces and shape into balls. Flour your hands and flatten each ball into an oval shape by slapping it from one hand to the other and gently pulling it out. Try to keep the centre thinner than the rim of each nan.

To glaze, brush them with the beaten egg yolk and sprinkle with poppy or onion seeds. Remove the hot trays from the oven and grease them quickly with butter paper or oil. Place four nans on each tray and return to the oven. Bake for 10 minutes or so, until puffed up and golden. Keep them wrapped in a clean cloth until you are ready to serve.

The traditional clay baking produces dark spots on the breads. If you want to replicate this, put them under a hot grill for 1–2 minutes before serving. Nans freeze well and all you need to do is to defrost them, then wrap them in foil and reheat in a low oven.

CHAPPATIS AND POORIS

Unyeasted

Chappatis and pooris are unleavened breads served to accompany curries. They are made from the same dough but, whereas chappatis come out as flat, blistered pancakes, pooris are deep fried and come out like light fritters.

CHAPPATIS

Allow 1½–2 hours

Makes 10–12

   350g/12 oz white or wholemeal flour or a mixture
   1 tsp salt
   c. 200ml/⅓ pint water
   vegetable oil, for greasing
   concentrated butter or ghee (sold in Asian shops and
      some supermarkets)

Sift the flour and salt into a large mixing bowl, holding the sieve high over the bowl to incorporate as much air as possible. Add water gradually to make a soft dough. Cover and leave at room temperature for 1 hour.

Grease your palms with a little oil and knead the dough vigorously on a clean surface for 5 minutes or more.

Divide the dough into 10–12 pieces. Make each into a ball, then flatten it on a lightly floured board. Roll out to a circle about 18cm (7in) across, keeping the remaining dough covered so that it does not dry out.

Heat a griddle or heavy frying pan until smoking hot

43

and cook each chappati as you make it, on both sides, until brown spots appear. Brush immediately with ghee or butter and keep the cooked ones warm on a sheet of foil beside the griddle or pan, adding new ones as you cook them. Serve hot.

Cooked chappatis can be stacked in foil and frozen. To use, defrost and then warm them in a low oven, still wrapped, for 15 minutes or so.

POORIS

Allow 1½–2 hours

Makes 20–24

350g/12 oz white or wholemeal flour or a mixture
1 tsp salt
c. 200ml/⅓ pint water
oil, for deep frying

Make the same dough as for chappatis, allow it to rest for an hour and divide it into 20–24 balls, half the size of the chappatis. Roll each one out, keeping the others covered meanwhile.

Heat enough oil for deep frying (use a small deep frying pan with 2cm/1in of oil). When the oil is very hot, fry one poori at a time, tapping its edges with a wooden spatula to encourage it to puff out.

Put the cooked pooris in a bowl or colander lined with kitchen paper to drain the excess oil and keep them covered while you cook the rest. Serve hot.

MISSI ROTIS

Unyeasted
Gluten-free
Allow 1½–2 hours

These unleavened breads come from North India. Gram flour, from which they are made, is gluten-free and although many recipes add wheat flour to improve the rather dry texture of the chickpea gram, this version using all gram flour is very palatable.

Makes 6

230g/8 oz gram flour, plus extra for dusting
1 green chilli, deseeded and chopped, or ½ tsp chilli powder
½ onion, finely chopped
1 Tbsp chopped fresh coriander
½ tsp turmeric
½ tsp salt
1 Tbsp oil
c. 150ml/5fl oz warm water
2–3 Tbsp melted butter or ghee or oil

Mix the flour, chilli, onion, coriander, turmeric and salt together in a large bowl and stir in the tablespoon of oil. Mix in enough water to make a soft dough. Turn it out on to a gram-floured surface and knead until smooth. Leave to rest in a bowl covered with clingfilm for about 1 hour – this gives the flavours time to develop.

Turn the dough out again on to the floured surface. Divide it into 6 pieces and shape into balls. Roll each one into a round about 13–15cm (5–6in) across.

Heat a heavy based frying pan or griddle over medium

heat for a few minutes. Brush each roti in turn with some of the melted butter or ghee or oil and cook in the hot pan for a minute on each side – until it is just turning brown. Brush again when you take it out and keep warm on a plate in a low oven.

Serve the rotis warm. They make a delicious base for scrambled eggs, but, traditionally, they are eaten alongside curries.

Breads from around the world

British Isles

ENGLISH MUFFINS

Allow 2½–3 hours

As sold by the 'muffin man' in the traditional nursery rhyme. They should be re-toasted gently on both sides, then split and pulled apart rather than cut (the crumb will stay softer and absorb more butter). If you have an Aga, you could bake them for five minutes in the hot oven instead of toasting.

Makes 9–10

15g/½ oz fresh yeast or
 1 Tbsp Easyblend dried
 yeast
15g/½ oz caster sugar
300–350ml/10–12fl oz
 warm water or half
 water, half milk
450g/1lb strong white flour, plus extra for dusting
1 tsp salt
1 Tbsp melted butter
fine semolina, for dusting

> *Variation*
> Try using half white,
> half wholemeal flour
> or all wholemeal.

Crumble the yeast into a small bowl with the sugar and stir in the warm liquid. Leave about 10 minutes, until frothy.

Put the flour and salt into a large bowl, adding the Easyblend dried yeast now if using, and make a well in the middle. Melt the butter and then let it cool a little.

When the yeast mixture is lively, pour it into the flour

and add the melted butter. Mix well with your hand, stirring and then beating and kneading until smooth and elastic. This can be done either in the bowl, if it's big enough, or on a floured surface. When the dough is soft and smooth, cover it in the bowl with lightly oiled cling-film and leave in a warm place to double in size.

Turn the dough out on to the floured surface, knock back and knead for a couple more minutes. Roll it out until it is 1cm (½in) thick. Use a plain round cutter, about 8.5cm (3½in) diameter, dipped in flour, to cut out the muffins. You should get 9 or 10 muffins, gathering and rerolling the dough gently until it is all used. Flour a baking sheet, space the muffins on the sheet and dust with the fine semolina or more flour. Cover with a cloth and leave to prove in a warm place for 20–30 minutes.

Then, either grease a heavy based frying pan or griddle and warm over moderate heat, transfer the muffins to the pan in batches and cook for about 5 minutes on each side until golden brown, or leave them on the sheet and bake them in a 230°C/450°F/gas mark 8 oven for 10–15 minutes, turning them over after 5 minutes. Another option if you have an Aga, is to set the sheet directly on the bottom of the hot oven, which gives the toasting effect.

Cool on a wire rack. See above for how to eat.

THE ENGLISH COTTAGE LOAF

No added fat
Allow 3 hours

Makes 1 large loaf

    20g/¾ oz fresh yeast or 1 Tbsp Easyblend dried yeast
    400ml/14fl oz warm water
    675g/1½lbs strong white flour
    2 tsp salt

Grease 2 baking sheets (although you are making just 1 large loaf, you need 2 sheets for the proving stage).

Stir the fresh yeast into a cup of the warm water until dissolved. Mix the flour and salt in a large mixing bowl, then make a well in the middle. If using the Easyblend dried yeast, add it now. If not, pour the yeast mixture into the middle and mix to a firm dough, adding the remaining water as you need it. Aim at a fairly stiff dough. Knead it on a floured board for 8–10 minutes, until smooth and

English Cottage Loaf

springy. Return the dough to the bowl, cover with oiled clingfilm and leave to rise in a warm place for about 1 hour – it should have doubled in size.

Turn the dough out again on to the floured board, knock back and knead again for a minute or 2. Divide the dough into 2 balls – the first consisting of two thirds of the dough, the second of one third (weigh if in doubt as getting the proportions right is important). Place each ball on a prepared sheet. Cover with inverted bowls and leave in a warm place for about 20 minutes. *Do not overprove.*

Gently flatten the top of the large ball and the bottom of the smaller one. Cut a cross in the centre of the larger ball, about 3cm (1½in) across, brush with water and set the smaller ball on top. Now, using the first two fingers and thumbs of one hand, press a hole right down the middle of the 2 balls. Cover with oiled clingfilm and leave for about 10 minutes to recover, but not overprove. Turn the oven on to 425°F/220°C/gas mark 7 and set the bread in it while it heats up – the loaf will finish expanding in the increasing heat. Bake for 30–40 minutes, until well browned.

Cool on a rack.

This is a spectacular loaf, seldom made commercially nowadays because you cannot fit many in the oven at the same time.

IRISH SODA BREAD

Unyeasted
Allow 1 hour

This can be made with white, wholemeal or a mixture of flours.

Makes 1 loaf

225g/8 oz plain white flour (doesn't have to be 'strong')
225g/8 oz wholemeal flour
1 tsp salt
1 tsp bicarbonate of soda
1 tsp cream of tartar
1 tsp caster sugar
30g/1 oz butter or lard
350ml/12fl oz buttermilk or half yogurt, half water

Preheat the oven to 190°C/375°F/gas mark 5. Grease a baking sheet.

Sift all the dry ingredients into a large bowl, then rub in the butter or lard with your fingers. Mix in the liquid to make a soft dough but do not knead. Shape into a round, place on the baking sheet and mark the top with a large, deep cross. Dust with flour and bake for 35–40 minutes, until risen and nicely brown. Serve warm.

SCOTTISH BAPS

Allow 2½ hours

These are flat, soft rolls traditionally made for breakfast in Scotland, but equally good in a packed lunch.

Makes 8–10

25g/¾ oz fresh yeast or 1 Tbsp Easyblend dried yeast
300ml/½ pint warm milk and water, mixed half and half
450g/1lb strong white flour, plus extra for dusting
2 tsp salt
extra milk, for glazing

Grease and flour 2 baking sheets. Mix the fresh yeast with the warm milk and water. Sift the flour and salt together into a large bowl – mix in the Easyblend dried yeast at this point if using. Make a well in the centre and pour in the liquid. Mix to a soft dough, knead lightly in the bowl, cover with oiled clingfilm and leave to rise in a warm place for about 1 hour, until the dough has doubled in size.

Turn it out on to a floured surface and knock back. Divide the dough into 8–10 pieces, knead each one and roll out into a flattish round about 9cm (3½in) across. Repeat with the others. Transfer the baps to the prepared baking sheets, spacing them well apart, cover with oiled clingfilm or damp teacloths and leave to prove for about half an hour.

Meanwhile, preheat the oven to 200°C/400°F/gas mark 6. Press the centre of each roll gently with your middle fingers to prevent air blisters, brush the tops with milk and dust with flour. Bake for 15–20 minutes, until lightly browned. Dust them with a little more flour when you take them out of the oven and put them to cool on a wire rack. They are best eaten warm.

SCOTTISH BARLEY BANNOCKS

Unyeasted
Allow 30 minutes

Bannocks are flat, unleavened loaves cooked on a griddle on top of the stove. A large, heavy based frying pan can be used if you don't have a griddle. Barley flour can be bought at healthfood shops – it gives a good earthy flavour. This bread is delicious with butter and honey for tea.

Makes 4

> 115g/4 oz barley flour
> 55g/2 oz plain white flour
> ½ tsp salt
> ½ tsp cream of tartar
> 25g/1 oz butter or margarine
> 175ml/6fl oz buttermilk or half yogurt, half water
> ½ tsp bicarbonate of soda

Sift the flours, salt and cream of tartar into a large bowl. Rub in the butter or margarine. Mix together the buttermilk or yogurt mixture and bicarbonate of soda. When it bubbles, add it to the flour mixture and mix to a soft dough. Do not knead. Tip it out on to a floured surface and pat it until it forms a round about 1cm (½in) thick. Cut it into quarters.

Grease the griddle or frying pan and heat on top of the stove – use a moderate heat only or the outside will burn. Cook for 6–7 minutes per side, until they have browned and cooked through. Wrap in a cloth to keep them soft and eat while warm.

SCOTTISH BUTTERY ROWIES

Allow 3 hours from scratch

These small, crispy rolls from Aberdeen bear a strong resemblance to French croissants. They are not as rich, since the basic dough lacks the egg and milk of the croissant dough, but the main difference lies in the shape.

Makes 12–15

    450g/1lb risen white dough (see page 5)
    150g/5 oz butter, at room temperature
    60g/2½ oz lard, at room temperature

Flour 2 baking sheets.

Roll out the risen dough on a floured surface to form a rectangle 15 by 38cm (6 by 15in). Cream the butter and lard together and divide into 3 equal parts. Working from one end of the dough, dab a third of the butter and lard mixture over two thirds of the dough, not quite to the edges. Fold the plain bottom third of the dough up and the top third down over it. Half turn the dough and roll out again as above. Repeat the dabbing of butter and lard, the folding over and rolling out twice more, using all the butter and lard.

Roll the dough out again, to form a rectangle about 1cm (½in) thick. Cut it into small ovals or rounds or simply pull off rough lumps and place them well apart on the prepared baking sheets. Cover and put in a warm place (not *too* warm, though, or the fat will melt) to prove for about 20–30 minutes.

Meanwhile, preheat the oven to 200°C/400°F/gas mark 6. Bake the rowies for about 20 minutes, until nicely golden. Serve warm with home-made jam.

OATCAKES

Wheat-free
Gluten-free
Allow 30–40 minutes

These are simple and quick to make and can be baked in the oven if you don't have a heavy iron griddle or frying pan. The oatcakes are thin and delicate so handle them carefully.

Makes 8

230g/8 oz medium oatmeal, plus extra for dusting
1 tsp salt
pinch of bicarbonate of soda
25g/1 oz (scant) lard or other shortening, melted
c. 75ml/3fl oz boiling water

Mix the oatmeal, salt and bicarbonate of soda in a bowl. Stir in the melted lard or shortening and enough hot water to make a dough. Knead it with your fingers until smooth, turning it out on to a surface dusted with oatmeal. When it is easy to handle, divide the dough in half and roll out each half in turn into a thin round about ½cm (¼in) thick. Cut each round into quarters – called 'farls' in Scotland.

Lightly grease the griddle or frying pan (or baking sheet) and heat it over a moderate heat. Using a fish slice or other flat implement, lay the farls in the pan and cook for 4–5 minutes. Then turn them carefully and cook for 1–2 more minutes – they should not brown. Alternatively cook the second side under the grill for a minute, to save turning them. If you are baking them, cook them in a preheated 180°C/350°F/gas mark 4 oven for 15–20 minutes.

Cool on a wire rack. They are best eaten fresh, but will reheat if you want to crisp them up again. Store in an air-tight box or tin.

WELSH CLAY POT LOAVES

Allow 3–3½ hours

These loaves are the modern descendants of bread baked
by country people long ago in three-legged iron pots that
sat over a peat fire. Terracotta flower pots make for an
interesting shape and produce a good crust and an even
crumb.

This recipe is for two loaves – one made savoury with
onion, cheese and herbs, the other kept plain. You can, of
course, make both the same or invent your own variations.

You will need two clay pots 13.5cm (5½in) in diameter
and 12cm (4½in) deep, either new or scrubbed very well.
To temper them, oil them inside and out (use a pastry
brush and cooking oil), then bake them, empty, two or
three times in a 200°C/400°F/gas mark 6 oven for 30
minutes. You can do this when the oven is on for other

Welsh Clay Pot Loaf

food, over several days if this is more convenient. Once used, there's no need to temper them again.

Makes 2 loaves

450g/1lb flour, using a mixture of wholemeal, Granary and strong white
1½ tsp salt
15g/½ oz fresh yeast
280ml/10fl oz warm milk and water, mixed half and half
sesame seeds (optional)

For the Savoury loaf

25g/¾ oz butter
1 onion, finely chopped
100g/3 oz mature cheese, grated
chopped fresh herbs – thyme and marjoram perhaps

Grease the tempered pots and a large baking sheet. Sprinkle sesame seeds in the bottoms of the pots, if using.

If making the savoury version, melt the butter in a frying pan and soften the onion until golden. Set aside.

To make the dough, put the flours and salt into a large bowl, mix and make a well in the centre. Crumble in the yeast and mix in the warm water and milk gradually, to make a smooth, pliable dough. Knead on a floured surface for 8–10 minutes. Return the dough to the bowl, cover with oiled clingfilm and leave in a warm place for 1–2 hours, until doubled in bulk.

Knock back the risen dough, divide it into 2 and add the cooked onion, cheese and herbs to one half. Shape the dough into balls and set each in a prepared flower pot. They will half fill the pots. Cover with oiled clingfilm and leave to rise in a warm place until the dough is about

4cm (1½in) from the top. *Keep an eye on them* – over-rising at this stage will produce problems in the baking. Preheat the oven to 230°C/450°F/gas mark 8.

Now comes the fun. Invert the pots on to the baking sheet, side by side, leaving the pots in place over the dough. Bake them in the hot oven for 30 minutes (if they have over-risen, they will push the pots upwards and come out crooked), then slip them out of the pots, turn the oven down to 170°C/340°F/gas mark 3 and bake for another 10–15 minutes, to improve the crust and colour.

Cool on a wire rack.

Continental Europe

BAGUETTES

No added fat
Allow 7½–8 hours. Begin mid-morning for supper-time eating

French bakers use a mixture of strong white bread flour and 'farine fluide', which is a fine white plain flour, to make baguettes and they are baked in very hot, steamy ovens in order to achieve the crisp crust. However, you can still make good baguettes at home if you allow enough time for the dough to develop its flavour – it is much more delicious than the cheap supermarket imitations so often offered at parties. If you do buy baguettes, it is worth choosing the more expensive ones made with French dough. This recipe makes two medium length baguettes, but you can easily double it for a party. Note, though, that it is best if they are baked at the top of the oven, which may be difficult with four loaves.

Makes 2 medium baguettes

    300g/10 oz strong white flour
    150g/5 oz fine plain flour
    2 tsp salt
    10g/⅓ oz fresh yeast or 1 tsp Easyblend dried yeast
    300ml/10fl oz warm water

Measure the flours and salt into a large bowl. Sift half the flours and salt into another large bowl and add the crumbled fresh yeast or Easyblend dried yeast to this bowl. Then, beat in the warm water to make a batter.

Cover with oiled clingfilm and leave at room temperature for 3–4 hours to ferment and triple in size.

Then add the remaining flour gradually, beating with your hand until it is all incorporated into a soft dough. Turn the dough out on to a floured surface and knead for 8–10 minutes. Return the dough to one of the bowls, cover with oiled clingfilm and put in a warm place to rise for 1–2 hours – the dough will double in size.

Turn the dough out on to the floured surface and knock back. Divide it into 2 balls. Flatten each ball into a round, then fold the topside down and the bottom side up to meet in the middle, pressing to seal the edges. Do not hurry – resting the dough between handlings will help it not to tear.

Take each oblong piece of dough and gently stretch and roll it to make a loaf about 30cm (12in) long. Lay each stretched loaf between pleats on a floured tea towel (this helps it to hold its shape while proving). Cover with oiled clingfilm and leave to prove for about 1 hour.

Preheat the oven to 230°C/450°F/gas mark 9. Gently roll each proved loaf on to a greased baking sheet, spacing them well apart. Slash diagonally with a sharp knife, making 5 or 6 slits in each loaf. Put them on a high shelf in the oven and spray the inside of the oven with water (in a clean garden or household plant spray) 3 times in the first 5 minutes of baking. Bake for 20 minutes altogether.

Cool them on a wire rack and eat the same day.

CROISSANTS

Allow 4 hours when starting from scratch

Originally made by bakers in Budapest to celebrate a victory over the Turks (presumably to eat the shape of the Turkish emblem was to emphasise their superiority over the foe), these crescent-shaped flaky rolls are quite an effort to make but very delicious.

Makes 8 large or 16 small croissants

450g/1lb risen enriched white dough (½ quantity of basic recipe, page 9)
225g/8 oz butter, at room temperature

Glaze

1 egg yolk
1 Tbsp milk

Turn out the risen dough on to a floured surface, knock back and knead for 2–3 minutes. Then wrap in clingfilm and chill in the fridge for half an hour. Return it to the floured surface and roll out into a rectangle 17 by 40cm (7 by 17in). Divide the butter into 3 equal parts and dab one part over the top two thirds of dough, not quite to the edges. Fold up the bottom, plain, third and then the top third down over it.

Turn the dough through 90 degrees and roll out again to a rectangle the same size as before. Repeat the buttering, folding and the rolling and turning twice more until all the butter has been used up. After the final folding, wrap the dough in clingfilm and return it to the fridge to rest for half an hour. (You can freeze the dough at this stage.)

Finally, roll out the dough into a rectangle about 60 by 30cm (24 by 12in). Cut it in half lengthways and then crossways to form 8 squares the same size.

For large croissants, roll each square from one corner to the opposite one, then curve the ends into a crescent shape.

For small croissants, cut each square in half diagonally to form 2 triangles, then roll up each triangle from the base towards the point, curving the ends as before to make a crescent.

Place the croissants, well apart, point downwards, on 2 floured baking sheets. To glaze, beat the egg yolk and milk together and brush over the tops of the croissants. Cover and prove at room temperature for about 30 minutes, until light and puffy. Set the remaining glaze to one side.

Meanwhile, preheat the oven to 220°C/425°F/gas mark 7.

Brush the croissants a second time with the glaze, then bake for 15–20 minutes – swapping the sheets round at half-time – until crisp and golden.

Cool on a rack briefly, serving them warm.

BRIOCHE

Allow 15 hours – 3 + overnight + 3–4 hours

This buttery French favourite is so rich with eggs that it takes time to rise, but it is well worth the trouble. It's also worth buying or borrowing a large fluted brioche mould to make it in.

Makes 1 large loaf

- 15g/½ oz fresh yeast
- 4 Tbsp warm milk
- 350g/12 oz strong white flour
- ½ tsp salt
- 3 eggs, beaten
- 175g/6 oz unsalted butter, at room temperature
- 25g/1 oz caster sugar

Glaze

- 1 egg yolk
- 1 Tbsp milk

> *Variation*
>
> Make 10–12 small brioche, instead of 1 large one. You will need small dariole or brioche tins. Shape as for the large brioche, dividing the dough appropriately. Bake for 15–20 minutes.

Mix the yeast and warm milk together. Sift the flour and salt into a large bowl, make a well in the centre and stir in the yeast mixture and the beaten eggs to make a dough. Knead on a floured surface for a few minutes until smooth and elastic. Cream the butter and sugar together and add little by little to the dough, kneading each addition in. When all has been incorporated, the dough will be smooth and shiny. Put it in a bowl, cover with oiled clingfilm and leave in a warm place to rise

65

until doubled in size – this may take 2–3 hours.

Knock back the risen dough, then cover again and leave in the fridge either overnight or for 8 hours.

Butter a large brioche mould (1.5-litre/2½-pint capacity) thoroughly. Turn the cold dough out on to a floured surface. Cut off nearly a quarter of it and set aside. Shape the rest into a ball and place in the buttered mould. Shape the reserved dough into an elongated egg shape. Using 2 fingers and the thumb of one hand pressed together, make a deep hole in the centre of the dough ball. Then, push the long end of the egg shape gently into the hole.

To make the glaze, beat the egg yolk and milk together and brush it over the brioche. Cover with lightly oiled clingfilm and leave to prove in a warm place for 2 or more hours, until the dough reaches the rim of the mould. Set the remaining glaze to one side.

Meanwhile, preheat the oven to 230°C/450°F/gas mark 8. Brush the dough again with the remaining glaze before baking in the preheated oven for 10 minutes, then reduce the heat to 190°C/375°F/gas mark 5 for another 20–25 minutes, until well risen and golden.

Cool on a wire rack.

PAIN AUX NOIX (WALNUT BREAD)

Allow 2½–3 hours

When the French think of nuts, they think of walnuts – hence the simple 'noix'. This bread – enriched with eggs and milk as well as walnuts – makes a delicious accompaniment to strong-flavoured cheeses. The sultanas add a little moist sweetness, but, if you prefer, you can omit them and add a tablespoon of light brown sugar instead.

Makes 2 small loaves

450g/1lb wholemeal flour
1 tsp salt
20g/¾ oz fresh yeast or 1 Tbsp Easyblend dried yeast
225g/8fl oz warm milk
1 egg, beaten
120g/4 oz walnuts
60g/2 oz sultanas or raisins or 1 Tbsp light brown
   sugar
milk, for glazing

Mix the flour and salt in a large bowl. If using fresh yeast, make a well in the middle of the flour and crumble the yeast in to it. Pour on the warmed milk and mix to dissolve the yeast. If using Easyblend dried yeast, however, simply add it to the flour with the salt, make a well and mix in the warmed milk.

Add the beaten egg and use your hand to mix it all well together. You are aiming at quite a damp dough, but it will require 5 minutes of kneading on a floured surface.

When it is soft and supple, flatten it out and spread the nuts and fruit or sugar over the dough, pressing them in.

Then, fold up the dough and form it into a ball. Return it to the bowl, cover with oiled clingfilm and leave to rise in a warm place until it has doubled in size – 1–1½ hours.

Turn the dough out on to the floured surface again, knock back and knead gently. Divide it into 2 balls, place them well apart on an oiled warm baking sheet, cover with oiled clingfilm and leave in a warm place to prove for about 30 minutes. Preheat the oven to 220°C/425°F/gas mark 7.

Brush the loaves with milk to glaze, then bake them in the centre of the preheated oven for 30–35 minutes.

Cool on wire racks.

GRISSINI (ITALIAN BREADSTICKS)

Allow 2½ hours

Grissini are those long, dry breadsticks to nibble on before a meal or to give to small children to crunch or suck. Home-made ones have more taste than shop-bought ones and are easy to make, though shaping the sticks takes a little time. You could use wholemeal or Granary flour instead of white, or a mixture.

Makes 16–20

>   2 tsp salt
>   225g/8 oz strong white flour
>   2 Tbsp olive oil
>   15g/½ oz fresh yeast or 1 tsp Easyblend dried yeast
>   125ml/4½ fl oz warm water
>   sesame or poppy seeds, to decorate (optional)

Sift the flour and salt into a large bowl and make a well in the middle. Either crumble the fresh yeast into the well and add the water and olive oil gradually, creaming it in as you stir, or add the Easyblend dried yeast straight into the dry flour and then beat in the water and the olive oil. Mix all to a soft dough, then turn it out on to a floured surface and knead for 5–7 minutes, until smooth and springy.

Roll the dough out into a rectangle, about 15 by 20cm (6 by 8in) and leave it on the board, covered with oiled clingfilm, in a warm place to rise for an hour or more, until it has doubled in size.

Preheat the oven to 200°C/400°F/gas mark 6. Cut the risen dough in half lengthways and then cut each half into 8, 9 or 10 strips, 7cm (3in) wide. Pull each strip out lengthways until it becomes a long stick. Stretch them gently, rather than rolling them. Brush each stick lightly with water and sprinkle with sesame or poppy seeds or leave plain. Place a little apart on 1 or 2 greased baking sheets and, when all the sticks are made, bake them for 20–30 minutes, swapping the sheets around after 10 minutes and keeping an eye on them so that they brown through without burning.

Cool on a rack and store in a tall, airtight tin or spaghetti jar.

PANE BASSO (TUSCAN BREAD)

Tu proverai sì come sa di sale/Lo pane altrui . . .
You shall find out how salt is the taste of another
man's bread . . .
  Dante Alighieri, *Divina Comedia*, 'Paradiso' canto 17, 1. 58

No added fat
Salt-free
Allow 14 hours

Salt-free bread, unless you are on a special diet, is rare
these days as salt is a cheap commodity. In the past, when
salt taxes were high, salt-free bread was more common.
In Tuscany, the cured hams, salty olives and anchovies
compensate for the lack of salt in the bread that they
accompany. You need to start the bread the day before
you want to bake it to give the starter time to develop.

Makes 1 medium loaf

Starter

Allow 10 hours
120g/4 oz strong white flour
200ml/7fl oz boiling water

Dough

Allow 3½–4 hours
175ml/6fl oz warm water
15g/½ oz fresh yeast or 2 tsp Easyblend dried yeast
450g/1lb strong white flour

First, make the starter by putting the flour into a large

bowl and pouring the boiling water on to it, mixing well to form a batter. Cover with a damp cloth and leave overnight at warm room temperature.

Next day, to make the dough, add the warm water to the starter and crumble in the fresh yeast. (If using Easyblend dried yeast, mix that with the flour.) Add the flour to the starter and mix to a slack dough. Knead it in the bowl until smooth, then cover with oiled clingfilm and leave in a warm place to rise for 1–2 hours, until it has doubled in size.

Turn the dough out on to a floured surface, knock back and shape into a flattish round. Fold the sides into the centre and pinch them together to seal. Lay the loaf, seam side up, on a lightly floured baking sheet, cover with oiled clingfilm and leave in a warm place to prove until it has doubled in size – 30–40 minutes.

Lightly oil a second baking sheet, lay it carefully on top of the risen loaf and flip it and the other baking sheet over so that the floured side is uppermost. Remove the first baking sheet. Leave the loaf to recover for 20–30 minutes. Meanwhile, preheat the oven to 220°C/425°F/gas mark 7.

Slash the top of the loaf with a sharp knife, making 2 or 3 long cuts, then bake for 30–35 minutes until golden.

Cool on a wire rack.

CIABATTA

Allow 12 hours for the 'biga' and 3¼ hours for the rest of the recipe

This Italian bread, called after its slipper-like shape, is one of the most popular in Britain and is made by local bakeries and sold in every supermarket.

The olive oil produces a soft crumb and a chewy crust in this recipe. It is not altogether easy to make at home because the dough is much wetter than most and difficult to handle. Be brave and do not be tempted to add more flour. You will need some of the 'biga' starter described on page 14.

Makes 1 loaf

> 15g/½ oz fresh yeast or 2 tsp Easyblend dried yeast
> 200ml/7fl oz warm water
> 225g/8 oz 'biga' (page 14)
> 2 Tbsp warm milk
> 300g/10 oz strong white flour, plus extra for dusting
> 1 tsp salt
> 1 Tbsp olive oil

If using fresh yeast, mix it with the warm water and add this to the biga in a large bowl, mixing with your fingers to make a soup. Add the milk. Mix in the flour and salt (add the Easyblend dried yeast at this point, if using), then add the olive oil, beating with your hand to lift and stretch the dough. Keep it in the bowl as it will be too wet to knead in the usual way. Continue to beat the dough for at least 10 minutes, punching it down and lifting it up within the bowl. Cover the bowl with oiled clingfilm and leave the dough in a warm place to rise – it will take about 2 hours. It should rise well.

Meanwhile, prepare a large baking sheet by dusting it well with flour. Pour the soft, risen dough – there is no need to knock back – on to the baking sheet, then flour your hands and shape it into a large oblong, about 30 by 15cm (12 by 6in). Tuck the edges in to give it a good shape and sprinkle the loaf with flour. Leave it in a warm place to prove for about 30 minutes. It should spread and rise.

Preheat the oven to 230°C/450°F/gas mark 8. Bake the ciabatta for 20–25 minutes, until it is golden and sounds hollow when tapped on the base.

Cool on a wire rack.

Variations

Olive Ciabatta
Add 60g (2 oz) chopped black olives to the dough when you add the olive oil.

Tomato Ciabatta
Add 60g (2 oz) chopped sun-dried tomatoes, drained of their oil, to the dough when you add the olive oil.

FOCACCIA OR PIZZA BIANCA

Allow 3½ –4 hours

Flat hearth breads such as focaccia were traditionally cooked on the oven floor before the fire had settled for the main baking of the day. The dough is made using olive oil and more oil is sprinkled into the characteristic dimples before baking, giving it a lovely flavour and texture.

Makes 2 rounds or 1 rectangle

25g/1 oz fresh yeast or 1 Tbsp Easyblend dried yeast
325ml/11–12fl oz warm water
550g/1¼lb strong white flour
2 tsp salt
2–3 Tbsp olive oil

For the topping

more olive oil
fresh rosemary
sea salt

Oil 2 round 25-cm (10-in) pizza or shallow cake tins or a large rectangular baking sheet. Cream the fresh yeast into a little of the warm water, then stir in the rest of the water. Mix the flour and salt in a large bowl (add the Easyblend dried yeast at this point, if using). Make a well in the centre of the flour, add the fresh yeast mixture or just the warm water if using Easyblend dried yeast and mix to a dough. Add the olive oil and knead it well in.

Turn the dough out on to a floured surface and knead it until it is smooth and elastic – it will be quite a soft dough. Return the dough to the bowl, cover it with oiled clingfilm and leave in a warm place to rise until it has doubled in size – about 1–1½ hours.

Knock back the dough and turn it out on to the floured surface again. Divide it into 2 balls and place each in one of the prepared tins, flattening it out with your hand to spread the dough to the edges. If the dough keeps springing back towards the middle, let it rest for a few minutes and try again. Alternatively, put all the dough on to a rectangular baking sheet and spread it from the centre outwards. A straight-sided tumbler can be used to help you roll the dough towards the edges. Cover with oiled clingfilm and leave to rise again for 30 minutes.

Now use your fingertips to make deep dimples all over the dough, replace the clingfilm and leave to prove once again for about 1 hour, or until it has doubled in bulk. The dimples will look like small eyes in a fat face. Meanwhile, preheat the oven to 230°C/450°F/gas mark 8.

Drizzle the olive oil into the dimples and scatter with the sea salt crystals and sprigs of rosemary. Bake in the preheated oven for 20–25 minutes, swapping the tins round at half-time, until both are golden.

Cool on a wire rack, and eat while fresh.

Middle East

PITTA BREADS

Allow 1¾–2¼ hours

This Turkish bread, which forms a pocket as it cooks, is found all over the Middle East and in Western super-markets, too. Pittas freeze well and can easily be reheated under the grill or in a hot oven. They are perfect for quick meals, slit open and filled with salad, or, as in the streets of Tunis, with fried eggs and harissa (a hot, peppery sauce). You can make them oval or round, with white flour or a mixture of white and wholemeal.

Makes 8–10

> 15g/½ oz fresh yeast or 1 Tbsp Easyblend dried yeast
> 300ml/10fl oz warm water
> 450g/1lb strong white flour or ⅔ white, ⅓ wholemeal
> 2 tsp salt
> 1 Tbsp olive oil

If using fresh yeast, dissolve it in the warm water. Mix the flour and salt in a large bowl (if using Easyblend dried yeast, mix it with the flour now). Make a well in the centre and add the water and yeast mixture (or just warm water), and the olive oil, beating everything together to make a soft dough.

Turn the dough out on to a floured surface and knead vigorously for 5–10 minutes, until it is smooth and elastic and no longer sticks to your fingers. Return it to the bowl, cover with oiled clingfilm and leave in a warm place to double in size – about 1–1½ hours.

Knock back, knead again for a few minutes, then divide the dough into 8–10 pieces, each about the size of an egg. Lay oiled clingfilm over them while they rest for 5 minutes. Then, roll each one out into an oval about 5mm (¼in) thick. Lay them on a floured tea towel, cover with another floured tea towel and leave to prove for 20 minutes or so.

Meanwhile, preheat the oven to 230°C/450°F/gas mark 8 and heat 2 large, oiled baking sheets in the oven.

When the pittas have risen, lay them on the heated baking sheets, spaced apart, sprinkle lightly with cold water and bake for 4–6 minutes. They should puff up in the heat of the oven, but not colour. You will need to cook them in batches if they don't all fit on the trays at once.

Cool briefly on a wire rack, then wrap them in a tea-cloth or put them in a polythene bag to keep them soft until you serve them.

Russia

BLINIS

Gluten-free, if you use only buckwheat
Allow 2½–3 hours

Blinis are Russian pancakes made from buckwheat, which, in spite of its name, is not wheat at all but a member of the dock plant family. They are easy to make and delicious served with soured cream and caviar for special occasions.

This version uses half buckwheat, half plain flour: if you like the rather strong flavour, you can increase the proportion of buckwheat or use all buckwheat, which makes them gluten-free.

Makes 20–25 (10cm/4in diameter)

110g/4 oz buckwheat flour ⎱ or 225g/8 oz buck-
110g/4 oz strong white flour ⎰ wheat flour
1 tsp black pepper, freshly ground
1 tsp salt
15g/½ oz fresh yeast
415ml/¾ pint warm milk
2 eggs, separated

Serving tip

Caviar is not essential. Replace with tiny strips of anchovy on the soured cream, or pieces of smoked salmon or even cured ham (prosciutto).

Mix the flours, pepper and salt in a large bowl.

Put the yeast in a small bowl and stir in a little of the warm milk to make a cream. Gradually add the rest of the milk, stirring. Make a well in the middle of the flour mixture, put in the egg yolks and stir in the milk and yeast mixture to make a smoothish batter.

Cover the bowl with oiled clingfilm and leave in a warm place for about an hour. The mixture will begin to ferment and look bubbly.

Whisk the egg whites with a pinch of salt until stiff but not dry and fold them into the bubbly batter. Cover the bowl and leave to ferment again for about 1 hour.

Brush a heavy based large frying pan lightly with oil and heat it over a moderate heat. Using about 3 tablespoons of batter at a time, ladle the batter into the frying pan to form small rounds. As with crumpets, tiny holes will appear on the surface. Turn them with a palette knife to cook the other side and stack them on a clean cloth. Keep warm while you cook the rest of the blinis.

You can keep the batter overnight in the refrigerator if it is more convenient, removing it an hour before you need to make the blinis. Blinis reheat well in a moderate oven, stacked and covered with foil.

3

Teabreads

Not surprisingly, most of these recipes are British, though the recipe for Banana Bread shows West Indian influence.

Many teabreads are unyeasted, which cuts down on the preparation time required but means that they do not keep for long. The Fruit Tea Loaf and Banana Bread are exceptions to this rule – the fruit in them means that they remain moist and delicious for several days.

> You are offered a piece of bread and butter that feels like a damp handkerchief and sometimes, when cucumber is added to it, like a wet one.
>
> Sir Compton Mackenzie, *Vestal Fire*

SCONES

Unyeasted
Allow 45 minutes

To get a good rise, do not roll out too thin.

Makes 10–12

225g/8 oz self-raising
   flour
½ tsp salt
45g/1½ oz butter
1 Tbsp white sugar
   (optional)
150 ml/5fl oz milk

Cook's tip

Handle the dough as
lightly as possible to
avoid heavy scones.
Kneading is definitely
not required.

Preheat the oven to 200°C/450°F/gas mark 6.

Sift the flour and salt into a large bowl and rub in the butter with your fingertips until the mixture looks like breadcrumbs. Mix in the sugar, if using. Then, use a table knife to stir in the milk, cutting and turning until it forms a soft dough.

Turn the dough out on to a floured surface and roll it out lightly until it is about 2cm (¾in) thick – no thinner. Use sharp, fluted cutters, 3–4 cm (1½in) in diameter, to cut cleanly through the dough. Lift the rounds with a palette knife on to a greased baking sheet, leaving a little space between them. Gather up the remaining dough and roll it out again lightly until all is used. Bake the scones in the preheated oven for 10–15 minutes, until risen and golden brown.

DROP SCONES

Unyeasted
Allow 30 minutes

One of the simplest teabreads to cook, these are much appreciated by children coming home from school at teatime.

Makes 12–15

225g/8 oz self-raising flour
1 egg
2 tsp golden syrup
280ml/½ pint milk

Put the flour in to a large bowl, make a well in the middle, break in the egg, add the syrup and gradually pour in the milk, drawing in the flour from the sides as you beat the mixture to make a smooth batter.

Grease a heavy based frying pan or griddle and heat. Drop the batter in spoonfuls on to the pan. When they bubble on top, turn them over carefully with a palette knife. Remove when golden on both sides.

Keep in a clean cloth and eat while fresh with butter.

CRUMPETS AND PIKELETS

Allow 2½ hours

Crumpets are fun to make, watching the bubbles of gas bursting on the surface to give them their pitted texture, which holds melted butter so well. The gas comes from the combination of yeast and bicarbonate of soda, two raising agents at once

If you do not have proper crumpet rings, any metal rings, such as pastry cutters or egg-poaching rings, will do. You can cook the batter on the griddle without rings, which will make thinner pancakes, rather like drop scones, and these are known as 'pikelets' in Yorkshire. They will not be as holey as crumpets.

Makes 12–15

350g/12 oz strong white flour or half strong, half plain
15g/½ oz fresh yeast or 1½ tsp Easyblend dried yeast
350ml/12fl oz warm water
½ tsp bicarbonate of soda
2 tsp salt
150ml/¼ pint warm milk

Mix the flour or flours and the crumbled or Easyblend dried yeast together in a large bowl and add the warm water gradually to make a batter. Beat it well until it becomes smooth and elastic. Cover the bowl with clingfilm and leave in a warm place until it looks alive and bubbly – about 1–1½ hours.

Stir the bicarbonate of soda and salt into the warm milk and add to the batter, which should be slack and runny but elastic. Cover again and leave for another 30 minutes.

Heat a griddle or heavy based frying pan and grease the

surface. Grease the inside of the crumpet rings or substitutes and stand them on the griddle. Pour the batter into each ring until it is about 1cm (½in) deep and cook over a gentle heat for 5–8 minutes. You will see the mixture gradually dry out and bubbles form and then burst on the surface.

Lift the rings off the crumpets and, when the tops are quite dry, flip them over and cook the other side briefly–for 1–2 minutes. Repeat with the rest of the batter. Keep the cooked crumpets or pikelets wrapped in a cloth until cool.

To serve, toast each side, butter the holey side and stack in a pile on a deep plate to keep warm and allow the butter to soak down the pile. Serve hot.

UNYEASTED MALT BREAD

Allow 1½ hours

At a tasting, my guests preferred this to the yeasted version (page 88).

Makes 1 small loaf

75g/3 oz malt extract
50g/2 oz dark brown sugar
25g/1 oz butter
150ml/¼ pint milk
225g/8 oz wholewheat flour
2 tsp baking powder
¼ tsp salt
75g/3 oz sultanas

Preheat the oven to 160°C/325°F/gas mark 3 and grease and flour a small loaf tin.

Heat the malt extract, sugar and butter together in a small pan until the butter melts. Take the pan off the heat and stir in the milk to cool the mixture.

Sift the dry ingredients into a bowl and mix in the liquid. Stir in the sultanas, then pour the mixture into the prepared loaf tin and bake in the preheated oven for about 1 hour, until risen, golden and firm.

Serve in thin slices, buttered.

YEASTED MALT BREAD

Allow 2-3 hours

A dark, moist loaf that keeps well.

Makes 2 small loaves

20g/¾ oz fresh yeast
1 tsp sugar
450g/1lb wholewheat
  flour
½ tsp salt
250ml/9fl oz warm water
175g/6 oz malt extract
100g/4 oz black treacle
50g/2 oz butter
100g/4 oz sultanas

Glaze

50g/2 oz sugar
1 Tbsp water

> ### Cook's tip
> Weigh out sticky malt extract and black treacle by weighing the whole jar or tin and spooning out the required amount straight into the pan – simply subtract the amount needed from the weight of the whole jar.

Grease and flour 2 small loaf tins.

Prepare the yeast by mixing it with the sugar and 3 tablespoons of the warm water in a small bowl and leaving it in a warm place to froth up – about 10–15 minutes.

Warm the flour and salt in a large bowl.

Heat the malt extract, treacle and butter together until they just melt, then remove from the heat to cool slightly. Add this and the yeast mixture to the dry ingredients and stir in the sultanas.

Beat the mixture hard with a wooden spoon to stretch the gluten (it will be too sticky to mix by hand), then pour it into the 2 prepared tins. Cover and leave in a warm place to prove for 1–2 hours – they will rise a little.

Preheat the oven to 200°C/400°F/gas mark 6. Bake the loaves for 35–40 minutes. Meanwhile, make the glaze by stirring the sugar or water together in a small pan until the sugar dissolves. Boil for 2 minutes, then remove from the heat. Brush the loaves while hot with the sugar and water glaze.

WELSH BARA BRITH

Allow 3–3½ hours

This Welsh recipe makes a delicious light, fruity bread. Its name means 'speckled bread'. Most bread recipes that include fruit add it after the first rise, but I find it easier to mix it in at the beginning with the sugar and spice. It takes a little longer to rise, but the result is good.

Makes 1 large loaf

20g/¾ oz fresh yeast or 1 Tbsp Easyblend dried yeast
240ml/8fl oz warm milk
1 egg
500g/1lb 2 oz strong white flour
75g/3 oz butter or lard
½ tsp salt
1 tsp ground mixed spice
50g/2 oz soft brown sugar
260g/9 oz mixed dried fruit and peel or just currants

Glaze

50g/2 oz honey or caster sugar
1 Tbsp water

Dissolve the fresh yeast in 2 tablespoons of the warm milk and keep in a warm place.

Beat the egg into the remaining milk. Put the flour into a large bowl and rub in the butter or lard with your fingertips until the mixture looks like breadcrumbs. Stir the salt, mixed spice, sugar and fruit into the flour. Add the Easyblend dried yeast now, if using. Make a well in the centre and pour in the yeast and milk and egg mixtures to make a rough dough, adding more flour if it's too sticky to handle.

Turn the dough out on to a floured surface and knead until smooth and elastic. Shape into a ball and place in a large bowl and cover with oiled clingfilm, then put it in a warm place until it has doubled in size – 1–2 hours.

Turn the dough out again on to the floured surface, knock back and knead for a couple of minutes. Then, either put it into a greased large, round, deep cake tin or shape it into a round and place it on a greased baking sheet. Cover with oiled clingfilm and leave in a warm place to prove until well risen.

Preheat the oven to 200°C/400°F/gas mark 6 and bake for 30–40 minutes. Keep an eye on it and if the top browns too quickly, cover it with foil for the final 10 minutes.

To make the glaze, put the honey or sugar and water in a small saucepan, stir to dissolve, and bring to the boil. Boil for 2 minutes. Place the hot loaf on a wire rack and brush the top with the glaze.

WILTSHIRE LARDY CAKE

Allow 3 hours if making from scratch

Makes 1 square loaf

450g /1lb ordinary white bread dough (see recipe, page 5, following steps to just after 1st rise, when it has doubled in size)
175g/6 oz lard, at room temperature
175g/6 oz mixed dried fruit
50g/2 oz mixed peel
175g/6 oz granulated sugar

Glaze

50g/2 oz caster sugar
1 Tbsp water

Roll out the dough on a well-floured surface to about ½cm (¼in) thick. Spread with half the lard, fruit, peel and sugar. Fold it in three, press the ends down with the rolling pin, give it a half turn and roll it out again.

Spread with the rest of the lard, fruit, peel and sugar. Roll the dough out to form a square 2cm (1in) thick. Place it in a square deep tin measuring 23 x 23 x 5cm (9 x 9 x 2in), cover it with a cloth or oiled clingfilm and leave to rise in a warm place for 20–30 minutes. Preheat the oven to 215°C/425°F/gas mark 7.

To make the glaze, put the sugar and water in a small saucepan, stir over a low heat to dissolve the sugar, then boil for 2 minutes. Score the top with a knife and brush with the glaze, if using. Bake in the preheated oven for 30–40 minutes. Eat it while still warm, in thick, sticky slices.

FRUIT TEA LOAF

Unyeasted
Allow 6–10 hours to soak the fruit
Allow 1 hour 45 minutes to make the loaf

A good standby, this loaf improves if you keep it for a few days before eating. Unless your tin is non-stick, line the bottom with non-stick baking parchment.

Makes 1 large loaf

350g/12 oz mixed dried
   fruit and peel
120g/4 oz dark brown
   sugar
225ml/8fl oz cold Indian
   tea
1 egg
225g/8 oz self-raising flour

> **Cook's tip**
> Remember to keep tea left over from breakfast or teatime.

Put the fruit, peel, sugar and tea into a large bowl to soak for 6 hours or overnight.

Grease a large loaf tin and preheat the oven to 180°C/350°F/gas mark 4. Beat the egg and then the flour into the soaked fruit and pour the mixture into the prepared loaf tin. Bake in the preheated oven for 1 hour, then lower the temperature to 160°C/325°F/gas mark 3 and bake for another half an hour.

Cool on a rack.

The flavour is best if the loaf is kept for 2–3 days in an airtight tin or wrapped in clingfilm in the fridge. Serve thinly sliced and thickly buttered.

CHELSEA BUNS

Allow 3 hours

These sticky, sweet, coiled fruit buns are fun to make and very popular with children, both to make and eat.

Makes 12–18

450g/1lb strong white flour, plus extra, if required
125g/4 oz granulated sugar
grated zest of 1 lemon
125g/4 oz butter
100ml/2–3fl oz milk, plus extra, if required
2 eggs
30g/1 oz fresh yeast
125g/4 oz currants

Glaze

50g/2 oz sugar
2 Tbsp milk

To make the buns, put the flour into a large bowl with half the sugar, add the lemon zest and mix well.

Melt half the butter, let it cool a little, then mix with the milk and beat in the eggs. Cream the yeast in a little warm water.

Make a well in the flour mixture and gradually add the yeast and butter, milk and egg mixtures, stirring it all by hand to make a soft dough. Add a little more milk if it is too dry or more flour if it is too wet. Knead the dough well on a floured surface, then return it to the bowl, cover with oiled clingfilm and leave to rise in a warm place for about 1 hour, until it has doubled in size.

Knock back the dough on the floured surface and roll it out into a rectangle about ½cm (¼in) thick and three times as long as it is wide. Spread the rest of the butter over it and sprinkle the currants and rest of the sugar on top. Fold the right-hand third of the long side over to the left, leaving a third uncovered. Fold that left-hand third over the right-hand third to make a square, turn it and roll it out the other way to make a rectangle again.

Fold in the ends in the same way once more to make a square, then roll this up into a long sausage. Cut it into slices – the thickness being determined by how big you want the buns (note, though, that they double in size in the proving and baking stages) and lay these on a greased baking sheet, cut side up, almost touching each other. Cover with oiled clingfilm and leave to prove for 30–40 minutes. This proving at close quarters gives the buns their characteristic square shape.

Preheat the oven to 200°C/425°F/gas mark 7. Bake the buns in the centre of the oven for 20–30 minutes, until they are golden but not burned.

To make the glaze, dissolve the sugar in the milk over a low heat, then boil for 2 minutes to thicken. Brush the buns with the glaze as soon as you remove them from the oven, then cool on a wire rack.

BANANA BREAD

Unyeasted
Allow 1½ hours

We often have over-ripe bananas left in the bowl and this is the best use for them.

Makes 1 large loaf

350g/12 oz self-raising flour
½ tsp salt
75g/3 oz soft margarine
75g/3 oz soft brown sugar
75g/3 oz walnuts, chopped
3 ripe bananas
130g/5 oz golden syrup
2 eggs

Grease a large loaf tin well with oil or lard. Preheat the oven to 180°C/350°F/gas mark 4.

Sift the flour and salt into a large bowl and rub in the margarine until the mixture looks like breadcrumbs, then add the sugar and chopped nuts.

Mash the bananas with the golden syrup in a wide soup plate and then beat in the eggs. Stir this mixture into the dry ingredients and mix well. Turn into the prepared tin and bake in the preheated oven for about 1 hour. Test to see if the middle is done by inserting a skewer – it should come out clean.

Cool in the tin, then serve, sliced, with butter. It will keep in the fridge, wrapped in clingfilm, for several days.

4

Festival breads

Festivals call for celebration: we wear our best clothes and produce our best food. So this chapter has rich, spicy, colourful recipes for the major Christian festivals of

Christopsomo

Christmas and Easter. You will also find Lenten recipes –
Hot Cross Buns and Pretzels – a Harvest Sheaf and a recipe
for Prosphora, Greek Orthodox Altar Bread. The Jewish
sabbath bread – Challah – is also included.

DANISH JULEKAGE (FOR YULETIDE)

Allow 4½–5 hours

This sweet festive bread is fragrant with cardamom seeds and bright glacé fruits, but is still more of a bread than a cake. It is excellent served lightly buttered at breakfast or coffee time. The rich, eggy dough needs time to rise – especially once the fruit has been mixed in – so don't make it when you are in a hurry. You can vary the fruits used, so long as the total weight of fruit does not exceed the 200g (8 oz) of the recipe. This amount will fit a loaf tin, 23 by 13cm (9 by 5in).

Makes 1 large loaf

- 25g/1 oz fresh yeast
- 5 Tbsp warm milk
- 450g/1lb strong white flour, plus extra for dusting
- 2 tsp salt
- 75g/3 oz butter
- 12 cardamom pods (c. 1½ tsp seeds)
- ½ tsp vanilla essence
- 50g/2 oz light brown soft sugar
- grated zest of ½ a lemon
- 2 eggs, lightly beaten
- 225g/8 oz glacé and dried fruit (red, green and yellow cherries, pineapple, stem ginger, papaya, ready-to-eat dried apricots, dates, candied peel – choose for colour as well as taste and variety)

Glaze

- 1 egg white
- 2 tsp water

Topping

1 Tbsp caster sugar
½ tsp cinnamon
8 walnuts or pecan nuts (optional)

To make the loaf, put the yeast into a small bowl and blend in the milk.

Mix the flour and salt in a large bowl and rub in the butter with your fingertips. Make a well in the middle and pour in the yeast mixture, stirring in enough of the surrounding flour to make a thick batter. Sprinkle with a little more of the flour and set aside in a warm place to 'sponge' (a term bakers use to describe when the flour and yeast mixture comes alive and looks spongy on top) for 15–20 minutes.

Take the seeds from the cardamom pods and crush them in a mortar. Add them to the flour with the vanilla essence, soft sugar, lemon zest and beaten eggs and stir it all to make a softish dough.

Turn the dough out on to a floured surface and knead for 6–8 minutes, until it is smooth and elastic. Return it to the bowl, cover with oiled clingfilm and put in a warm place to rise and double its size, which may take 1½–2 hours.

Meanwhile, lay the glacé and dried fruit on the floured surface, sprinkle with more flour and chop, but not too finely (the flour stops it all sticking together).

Grease a large loaf tin.

When the dough is well risen, turn it out and knock back. With the palms of your hands, flatten it into a rectangle and spread half the chopped fruit over it. Fold the sides to the centre and then fold in half.

Flatten it again to form a rectangle and repeat with the rest of the fruit, folding and kneading to distribute it right through the dough. Return the dough to the bowl, cover and leave to rest for 15 minutes.

Now, roll the dough into a rectangle approximately 38 by 25cm (15 by 10in). Lay it with the short sides at the top and bottom, fold the bottom third up and the top third down, tuck in the sides and you should have a loaf that fits your prepared tin. Put it, seam side down, in the tin, cover with oiled clingfilm and leave to rise in a warm place for about 1 hour, until the dough reaches the top of the tin. Preheat the oven to 180°C/350°F/gas mark 4.

Slash the top of the loaf lengthways and then with diagonal cuts on each side. To make the glaze, mix the egg white with the water and brush over the top. For the topping, mix the sugar and cinnamon and sprinkle over the loaf, then, if using, arrange the nuts on top. Bake in the preheated oven for 35–45 minutes, but check after 20 minutes and, if the top is beginning to burn, lay some foil loosely over it.

Turn out and cool on a wire rack, top side up.

GERMAN STOLLEN

Allow 4½–5½ hours

This famous German bread is made at Christmas. Some say that the shape of the bread, folded over the marzipan filling, represents baby Jesus wrapped in swaddling clothes.

It is best to use fresh yeast for this egg- and fruit-enriched recipe.

Makes 1 large loaf

50g/2 oz currants
50g/2 oz sultanas
3 Tbsp rum or brandy or plum brandy
350g/12 oz strong white flour
½ tsp salt
grated zest of 1 lemon
50g/2 oz caster sugar
½ tsp ground cinnamon
½ tsp ground cardamom
30g/1 oz fresh yeast
115ml/4fl oz warm milk
50g/2 oz butter, melted
1 egg, lightly beaten
50g/2 oz chopped mixed peel
25g/1 oz chopped blanched almonds
icing sugar, for dusting

Marzipan filling

150g/6 oz ground almonds
50g/2 oz caster sugar
50g/2 oz icing sugar

2 tsp lemon juice
1 small egg, lightly beaten

Put the currants and sultanas in a small bowl with the rum or brandy and set in a warm place to swell.

Sift the flour and salt into a large bowl and stir in the lemon zest, sugar and spices. Cream the yeast with the warm milk in a small bowl. Make a well in the flour mixture, pour in the yeast mixture and incorporate a little of the flour to make a thick batter. Sprinkle the batter with some more of the flour, then cover with oiled clingfilm and leave in a warm place to 'sponge' (see page 100) for 30 minutes.

When it is nicely frothy, stir in the melted butter and beaten egg and mix to a soft dough with a wooden spoon. Then, turn it out on to a floured surface and knead with your hand for 6–8 minutes, until it is smooth and springy. Put the dough into a lightly oiled bowl, cover it with oiled clingfilm and leave in a warm place to rise – it may take 2 or even 3 hours to double in size.

Meanwhile, make the marzipan. Mix the ground almonds and sugars together in a bowl, stir in the lemon juice and enough egg to mix to a stiff paste. Knead it until it is smooth, then shape it into a long sausage between your hands and set aside, covered with clingfilm to prevent it from drying out.

When the dough is well risen, turn it out on to a floured surface and knock back. Flatten it into a rectangle about 1cm (½in) thick and scatter over it the soaked currants and sultanas, the peel and the chopped almonds. Fold the dough over and press and knead the dough until the fruits and nuts are mixed evenly through. Roll it out into a rectangle approximately 30 by 23cm (12 by 9in), leaving the centre thinner than the edges.

Lay the marzipan sausage along the centre of the dough and fold the dough over the marzipan, leaving the top edge short of the base so that the fold is visible. Press to seal the fold. Place on a greased baking sheet, fold side up, cover with oiled clingfilm and leave to prove for 40–60 minutes, until it has doubled in size again.

Meanwhile, preheat the oven to 200°C/400°F/gas mark 6.

Remove the clingfilm, then bake in the centre of the preheated oven for 30 minutes, or until it is nicely golden and sounds hollow on the bottom when tapped.

Cool on a wire rack. Dust with icing sugar when ready to serve.

CHRISTOPSOMO (GREEK CHRISTMAS BREAD)

Allow 4–4½ hours

Holidaymakers in Greece will know that 'psomi' means bread, so 'Christopsomo' means 'Christbread'. It is marked by a lovely Byzantine cross which is flavoured with aniseed and end-stopped with walnuts. Its light, buttery dough is spiced with cinnamon, cloves and orange zest.

Makes 1 large loaf

- 15g/½ oz fresh yeast
- 140ml/¼ pint lukewarm milk
- 450g/1lb strong white flour
- 2 eggs
- 75g/3 oz caster sugar
- ½ tsp salt
- 75g/3 oz butter, softened
- grated zest of ½ an orange
- 1 tsp ground cinnamon
- ¼ tsp ground cloves
- pinch crushed aniseed
- 8 walnut halves
- a little beaten egg white, for glazing

In a large bowl, mix the yeast with the lukewarm milk until smooth, then stir in 115g (4 oz) of the flour to make a batter. Cover with clingfilm and leave in a warm place to 'sponge' (see page 100) for about 30 minutes.

Beat the eggs and sugar together until light and fluffy. Beat them into the bubbly yeast mixture and then gradually add the rest of the flour and the salt. Beat in the softened butter and mix to a soft dough.

Turn the dough out on to a floured surface and knead for 5–10 minutes, until smooth and elastic. Return it to the bowl, cover with oiled clingfilm and leave in a warm place to rise for about 1½ hours, until doubled in size.

Grease a baking sheet. Turn the dough out again on to the floured surface and gently knock back.

Cut off a small piece of dough – about 50g (2 oz) – and set aside for the cross.

Gently knead the orange zest, cinnamon and cloves into the large piece of dough and shape it into a round loaf. Place it on the prepared baking sheet.

Mix the aniseed into the small piece of dough with your fingertips. Cut it in half and roll each piece into a long rope, much as you used to roll Plasticine or play dough as a child. Aim at making each one 30cm (12in) long.

Lay the 2 ropes in a cross on top of the loaf. Then, snip each rope-end lengthways towards the middle, to one-third of its length, leaving 2 thin strands. Curl these away from each other in Byzantine circles (as illustrated below). Place a walnut half in each circle.

Cover the loaf with oiled clingfilm and leave in a warm place to double in size – 30–40 minutes. Meanwhile, pre-heat the oven to 190°C/375°F/gas mark 5.

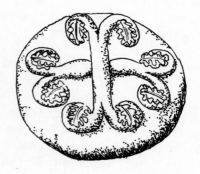

Brush the loaf with the egg white and bake in the pre-heated oven for 30–40 minutes, keeping an eye on it towards the end as it burns quickly.

Cool on a wire rack.

PANETTONE

Allow 4½–5 hours

This tall Italian Christmas loaf is very light, in spite of the butter and eggs and fruit. The larger than usual quantity of yeast helps the rich dough to rise. It also keeps well so can be brought out to offer to guests throughout the Christmas season – cut long, thin slices and enjoy with a glass of wine or vin santo.

Makes 1 large loaf

400g/14 oz strong white flour
1 tsp salt
50g/2 oz caster sugar
20g/¾ oz fresh yeast
120ml/4fl oz lukewarm milk
1 whole egg, beaten
2 egg yolks
120g/4 oz butter, softened
50g/2 oz sultanas
50g/2 oz raisins
50g/2 oz mixed chopped peel
25g/1 oz melted butter, for glazing

First, find a deep cake tin about 15–17cm (6–7in) across, then butter and line it with non-stick baking parchment or greaseproof paper, leaving a cuff of paper about 8cm (3in) above the rim of the tin.

Sift the flour and salt into a large bowl and stir in the sugar. Make a well in the centre, crumble in the yeast and add the milk, creaming the fresh yeast in gradually. Then mix in the whole egg, drawing in enough flour to make a thick batter in the middle of the bowl. Sprinkle it lightly with some of the surrounding flour and leave in a warm place to 'sponge' for half an hour or so.

When the batter looks bubbly and alive, add the egg yolks and mix in the rest of the flour to make a soft dough. Work in small pieces of the softened butter until it is all incorporated. Then, turn the dough out on to a floured surface and knead until it is smooth and elastic. Return it to the bowl, cover with oiled clingfilm and leave to rise at comfortable room temperature – no warmer – until the dough has doubled in size – 1–2 hours. If you put it in too warm a place, the butter will make the dough greasy.

Knock back the risen dough and turn it out on to the floured surface again to knead in the dried fruit and peel. Do this gradually, making sure that it is evenly distributed throughout the dough. Shape it into a ball and put it in the prepared cake tin. Cover with oiled clingfilm (balanced over the paper cuff) and leave to rise again at room temperature until it has doubled in height – about 1 hour.

Meanwhile, preheat the oven to 190°C/375°F/gas mark 5.

Brush the top of the loaf with some of the melted butter and use a sharp knife to cut a cross in the top. Bake in the preheated oven for 20 minutes, then turn down the heat to 180°C/350°F/gas mark 4. Brush with the melted butter again and bake for 30 minutes more, until a deep golden colour. Cool in the tin for 10 minutes, then turn the loaf out and cool on a wire rack – the right way up, so as not to flatten the dome.

Festival breads

PRETZELS AND BAGELS

Allow 2½–3 hours

Early Christians are said to have made bread shaped like pretzels in Lent – the ends crossed in the centre of the pretzel reminding them of the cross of Christ. The name itself comes from the Latin 'bracellae', which means 'little arms'. We think of pretzels and bagels as Jewish; they were brought to America by German immigrants in the nineteenth century and have become a staple of Jewish communities in the USA.

I give the recipes together here because they are so similar. The dough for each is poached briefly before baking, which gives them their chewy texture. This recipe makes eight pretzels, which fit on to one large baking sheet, but you could easily double the quantity if you need more.

PRETZELS

Makes 8 pretzels or bagels

225g/8 oz strong white flour
½ tsp salt
8g/¼ oz fresh yeast or 1 tsp Easyblend dried yeast
100ml/3½fl oz warm water
45ml/1½fl oz warm milk
15g/½ oz butter, melted

> These are bread pretzels, not the hard, crisp, salty biscuits sometimes served with drinks.

Glaze and topping

½ egg, beaten
1 Tbsp milk

sea salt crystals
caraway seeds

Put the flour and salt in a large bowl, mix and make a well in the middle. If you are using fresh yeast, crumble it into the well and stir the warm water and milk in gradually. If you are using Easyblend dried yeast, mix it into the flour before adding the liquid. Mix to a dough, adding the melted butter.

Turn the dough out on to a floured surface and knead for 4–5 minutes, until smooth and springy. Return it to the bowl, cover with oiled clingfilm and leave in a warm place to double in size – about 45–60 minutes.

Turn the dough out again on to the floured surface, knock down and knead for a few minutes. Divide the dough into 8 pieces, form them into balls and cover them with a cloth while you shape each one in turn.

On a well-floured surface, roll each ball into a long snake – at least 30cm (12in) – thinner at the ends than in the middle. Bend the snake into a horseshoe shape, then bring the ends back to the sides of the horseshoe, crossing over each other and looping them on the way (see illustration). Repeat until all the balls are shaped.

Preheat the oven to 190°C/375°F/gas mark 5. Beat the egg and milk together to make the glaze. Grease a baking sheet. Bring a large pan of salted water to the boil, then

turn it down to a simmer. With a slotted fish slice or spoon, lower the pretzels, 2 or 3 at a time, into the water and poach for about 1 minute.

Remove on to a clean cloth to drain, repeating the process until all the pretzels have been poached.

Transfer them to the prepared baking sheet, spacing them apart, and brush with the egg and milk glaze. Sprinkle each with sea salt or caraway seeds and bake until golden brown – about 25 minutes.

Cool on a rack.

BAGELS

Bagels are made in the same way as pretzels, with the following changes:

- omit the milk, replacing it with the same amount of water, adding 2 tsp malt extract and 1 Tbsp oil with the water

Bagels and Challah

- shape the dough into balls and then push a hole through the middle of each one with your thumb, enlarging the hole to allow for it to shrink as the dough rises
- add 1 Tbsp malt extract to the water before poaching the bagels
- glaze and sprinkle with poppy, sesame or caraway seeds, if you like, then bake as for pretzels.

CHALLAH

Allow 3–3½ hours

This is a Jewish plaited bread made for the sabbath. In Orthodox families, traditional blessings are said over the bread before it is broken and distributed, representing the manna sent by God to feed the Israelites on their journey from Egypt.

Makes 1 large or 2 small loaves

450g/1lb strong white flour
1 tsp salt
1 Tbsp white sugar
15g/½ oz fresh yeast or 2 tsp Easyblend dried yeast
200ml/7fl oz warm water
2 eggs, beaten
75g/3 oz butter or margarine, melted and cooled

Glaze and topping

2 tsp egg reserved from the 2 used above
2 tsp water
poppy seeds, to decorate

Grease a baking sheet. Sift the flour and salt into a large bowl, then add the sugar, mix and make a well in the centre. Crumble the fresh yeast into the well or, if using Easyblend dried yeast, mix it straight into the flour. Add the warm water and most of the beaten egg (see glaze ingredients above) gradually to make a soft dough, adding the melted butter or margarine as you go.

Turn the dough out on to a floured surface and knead until it is smooth and elastic. Return it to the bowl, cover with lightly oiled clingfilm and leave to rise in a warm place until it has doubled in size – about 1 hour or maybe more as the mixture is a rich one.

Knock back and knead again for a few minutes.

For 2 loaves

Divide the dough in two, then roll each half into 3 long ropes. Join the 3 ropes at one end and plait as usual, left and right alternately, tucking the ends under. Repeat for the second loaf.

For 1 loaf

Divide the dough into 4 pieces, rolling them into 4 ropes about 45cm (18in) long. Line them up and join them at one end. Starting from the right, lift the first rope over the second and the third over the fourth. Then, place the fourth rope between the first and second. Start again from the right and repeat the process until the plait is complete. Tuck the ends well under.

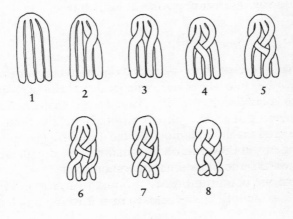

Lift the loaves or loaf on to the prepared baking sheet. Cover with oiled clingfilm and leave in a warm place to rise again for 30–40 minutes. Preheat the oven to 200°C/ 400°F/gas mark 6.

Mix the reserved egg with the water and brush over the loaves or loaf. Sprinkle with poppy seeds and bake in the preheated oven for 30–40 minutes (the smaller loaves will bake more quickly), until a rich golden colour.

Cool on a wire rack.

Delicious for breakfast or tea and as toast the next day.

The quick method

To minimise work on the sabbath, some Jewish cookbooks alter the sequence slightly, as follows.

Mix and knead the dough as above, but, instead of leaving it to rise the first time, divide and roll it into strands straight on to the baking sheet, brush the plaited loaves with water, slip the whole sheet into an oiled polythene bag and leave in the refrigerator overnight. Then, all you need to do the next day is take out the baking sheet, make sure the loaves have doubled in size, brush them with egg glaze, sprinkle with poppy seeds and bake as above.

Taking Challah

A small piece of the unbaked dough is removed, the following blessing is recited over it and then the piece of dough is burned.

> Blessed art thou Lord our God
> King of the Universe who sanctified
> us with his commandments and ordered
> us to set apart the Bread.
>
> *Jewish Prayer Book*

HOT CROSS BUNS

Allow 3½ hours or 20 minutes + overnight + 1½ hours next morning

These are one of the few recognisably Christian foods still commonly eaten in the UK. The fact that supermarkets stock them all year round should not deter us from making them for Good Friday. If you eat little else that day, you will find them real food for thought.

I find it most convenient to mix the dough the night before, leave it to rise slowly in the fridge or a cool larder and work through the final stages of knocking down, shaping, proving and baking the next morning. I use Easyblend dried yeast, but, if you use fresh or ordinary dried yeast, follow your usual method, letting it begin to froth in some of the warm liquid first.

Makes 12–18

450g/1lb strong plain flour
½ tsp salt
1 tsp mixed spice
1 tsp cinnamon
½ tsp grated nutmeg
½ tsp freshly ground mace
50g/2 oz caster sugar
1 level Tbsp Easyblend dried yeast
1 egg, beaten
110ml/4fl oz cold milk mixed with 110ml/4fl oz boiling water
50g/2 oz butter, melted and cooled slightly
100g/4 oz currants or raisins
50g/2 oz mixed peel

For the crosses

50g/2 oz flour
2–3 Tbsp water

Glaze

50g/2 oz granulated sugar
4 Tbsp water

Mix the flour, salt, spices, sugar and yeast together in a large, warm bowl. Make a well in the middle and add the egg, the warm liquid, melted butter and the fruit and peel. Mix to a soft dough with a wooden spoon, then turn it out on to a floured surface and knead for 5–10 minutes, until you have a smooth, elastic dough, adding more flour as you go if need be.

Return the dough to the bowl and place it all in a large, oiled polythene bag. Leave in a warm place for 1–1½ hours if you want it to rise quickly or else in the fridge overnight (see above). It should double in size.

Turn the risen dough out again on to a floured surface, break it down and knead lightly. Roll it into a long sausage shape and slice it into discs, 12–18, depending on how big you want them. Shape them into round buns and place them on baking sheets lined with non-stick baking parchment, leaving room for spreading. Leave them covered with a cloth in a warm place to prove and preheat the oven to 230°C/450°F/gas mark 8.

For the crosses, I find the bakers' method best, though you can just slash a cross on top of each with a sharp knife if you prefer. Otherwise, mix the flour and water to a smooth, thickish paste and pour it into a paper piping bag (make a cone shape with greaseproof paper, leaving a decent hole at the pointed end).

Pipe a cross on each bun. Miraculously, the crosses remain white while the buns brown. Bake on a middle shelf in the preheated oven for 15 minutes, in batches if necessary.

Meanwhile, prepare the glaze. Dissolve the sugar in the water in a small pan over a low heat. Boil briskly for 2–3 minutes, until syrupy. Brush this over the hot buns as soon as you have taken them out of the oven and put them on a wire rack to cool. To reheat buns, put them in a moderate oven for 10 minutes.

Festival breads

LAMBROTSOMO (GREEK EASTER BREAD)

Allow 3–3½ hours

In Greek homes at Easter, this special, spiced dough enriched with eggs and butter is plaited, decorated with brightly coloured hard-boiled eggs and baked for the feast. Some bring their loaves to church to be blessed.

Makes 1 large loaf

450g/1lb strong white flour
½ tsp salt
1 tsp ground all spice
½ tsp ground cinnamon
½ tsp caraway seeds
20g/¾ oz fresh yeast
175ml/6fl oz lukewarm milk
50g/2 oz butter
40g/1½ oz caster sugar
2 eggs

> **Cook's tip**
>
> If the loaf browns too quickly, lay a piece of foil over it to protect the top during the last stage of baking.

Decoration

3 small eggs in their shells
1 Tbsp white wine vinegar
¼ tsp red or orange food colouring
1 tsp olive oil

Glaze

1 egg yolk
1 tsp clear honey
1 tsp water
25–50g/1–2 oz blanched, flaked almonds

Mix the flour, salt, all spice, cinnamon and caraway seeds together in a large bowl. Make a well in the centre and crumble in the fresh yeast. Add the lukewarm milk gradually, creaming the yeast and mixing in some of the flour.

Cream the butter and sugar together and beat in the eggs. Add this mixture to the yeast and flour, mixing it all into a dough with a wooden spoon. It will be quite sticky.

Flour your hand and turn the dough out on to a floured surface to knead for 4–6 minutes, until smooth and elastic, reflouring the surface and your hand as you go.

Return the dough to the bowl, cover with oiled clingfilm and set to rise in a warm place for 1½–2 hours, until it has doubled in size.

Meanwhile, prepare the decoration. Prick the rounded end of each egg first to save them cracking, then hard-boil them for 10 minutes. Drain the eggs. Mix the vinegar and dye in a small bowl, then roll the eggs in it until they are evenly coloured. Leave them on a wire rack to cool. When they are cold, rub them all over with the oil. Grease a baking sheet.

Knock back the risen dough and knead again for 1–2 minutes on your floured surface. Divide the dough into 3 equal pieces and roll each into a thick rope about 40–50cm (15–20in) long. Join them together at one end and plait quite loosely. Tuck the ends under.

Lift the plait on to the prepared baking sheet and push the coloured eggs down between the strands of the plait. Cover with oiled clingfilm and leave in a warm place to prove for 30–40 minutes, until it has almost doubled in size.

Preheat the oven to 190°C/375°F/gas mark 5. Mix the egg yolk, honey and water to make the glaze.

Brush the dough with the glaze (not the eggs), sprinkle

with the almonds and bake for 25–30 minutes, until it is golden and sounds hollow when tapped on the bottom.

Cool on a wire rack.

This is a spectacular loaf and the eggs remain edible.

PROSPHORA (GREEK ORTHODOX ALTAR BREAD)

> For we being many are one bread, and one body: for we
> are all partakers of that one bread.
>
> 1 Corinthians 10.17

No added fat
Allow 3½ hours

If you have had holidays in Greece, you may have seen
round wooden bread stamps for sale in tourist shops
among the wooden spoons and olivewood bowls. The
intricate carving on the flat side of the stamp is very attractive and you may – as we did many years ago – bring one
home with you. The incised characters:

I C - X

N I K A

stand for 'Christos Nika', which means 'Christ conquers'
and the stamped cross shape is cut out of the loaf for
use during the Orthodox liturgy. How, though, do you get
the stamped pattern to survive the rising of the bread –
won't it just disappear? Thanks to the Internet and my
classically-educated but also computer-literate husband, I
now know the answer and have evolved this recipe from
several downloaded.

To be really authentic, you should be an Orthodox sub-
deacon to make these loaves, but you could say the 'Bread
of Life' prayer (given at the end of the recipe) over the
dough as you knead it and light incense beside the proving
bowl.

Most recipes give large quantities for the ingredients so
that many altar breads can be made at a time, but I have
given enough for just one loaf, cooked in a cake tin 19cm
(7½in) in diameter and 3.5cm (1½in) deep.

Makes 1 small loaf

   350g/¾lb strong white flour, plus extra for kneading
      and stamping
   1 tsp salt
   2 tsp Easyblend dried yeast
   230ml/8fl oz warm water
   olive oil, for greasing and glazing

Mix the flour, salt and yeast together in a large bowl. Make a well in the middle and stir in the water gradually, mixing with your hand to make a soft dough.

Turn the dough out on to a floured surface and knead until it is smooth and pliable, adding more flour as necessary.

Return the dough to the bowl, cover with oiled clingfilm or a damp cloth and leave in a warm place to rise until it has doubled in size – 1½–2 hours.

Turn the risen dough out on to a floured surface and knock back to get the air bubbles out of it. Divide the dough in two, take one half and flatten it into a disc that is slightly smaller than your cake tin.

Grease the cake tin with olive oil and place the disc of dough in it. Roll out the second piece to form a disc that is slightly thinner and larger than the first. (These discs symbolise Heaven and Earth and the dual nature of Christ – God and Man).

Brush the top of the first disc and the bottom of the second disc with water and lay the second carefully over the first, trying not to trap too much air between them.

Now for the stamping. Flour the wooden seal and shake off any excess flour. Also flour the surface of the bread. Now, press the seal firmly down on to the loaf and keep it there long enough for you to say the Lord's Prayer in your own language. Remove the seal carefully.

Next, take a toothpick or thin skewer and prick deep holes at the corners of the cross in the middle of the seal and also decoratively around the edge.

Cover the tin with a clean cloth and leave to prove until the dough has risen well – about 20 minutes. Meanwhile preheat the oven to 200°C/400°F/gas mark 6.

Bake it in the lower part of the oven for 15–20 minutes, turning it round once to ensure that it cooks evenly. Remove when it has coloured nicely and sounds hollow when tapped on the bottom.

The pattern of the seal should be clear. You can brush olive oil around the edge of the loaf to finish if you like, but leave the stamped area unglazed. My loaf rose and split slightly in the middle. I don't think that matters, though it meant the top surface was not entirely flat.

Bread of Life prayer

O Lord Jesus Christ, only begotten son of the Eternal Father, who has said: Without me you can do nothing! O Lord, my God, with faith I accept your words. Help me, a sinner, to prepare the bread of offering, that the works of my hands may be acceptable at the holy table and may become through the works of thy Holy Spirit, the communion of thy most pure body for me and all thy people. In the name of the Father and of the Son and of the Holy Spirit. Amen

HARVEST SHEAF

> For as the rain cometh down, and the snow from heaven, and returneth not thither, but watereth the earth, and maketh it bring forth and bud, that it may give seed to the sower, and bread to the eater.
>
> Isaiah 55.10

Allow 4–5 hours

Many of us have wondered at the elaborate, golden loaves displayed in parish churches at harvest festivals. Are they for eating or just for display? How do the sheaves of corn look so real? Do they ever go mouldy?

In fact, it is not really difficult to make a harvest sheaf, but you do need nimble fingers and an hour's peace and quiet while you shape the stalks and ears of wheat. Ideally, get some children or grandchildren to help (five- to eight-year-olds rather than two- to four-year-olds though).

The dough is a basic white one and the deep golden colour comes from the egg wash used to glaze it.

Makes 1

    1kg/2lbs 2 oz strong white flour
    1 Tbsp salt
    15g/½ oz fresh yeast or 2 tsp Easyblend dried yeast
    450ml/16fl oz warm water

Glaze

    1 egg, beaten
    2 Tbsp milk

First, find your largest baking sheet and grease it. It should be at least 38 by 33cm (15 by 13in).

Sift the flour and salt into a large bowl and make a well in the centre. Crumble in the fresh or mix the Easyblend dried yeast straight into the flour and add the water gradually, to make a stiff dough. Turn it out on to a floured surface and knead for a good 10 minutes, until smooth and elastic. Return the dough to the bowl, cover it with lightly oiled clingfilm and leave in a warm place to rise until it has doubled in size – probably 1½–2 hours.

Turn the risen dough out on to the floured surface, knock back and shape into a ball. Cover once more with the oiled clingfilm and leave it to rest for 5–10 minutes.

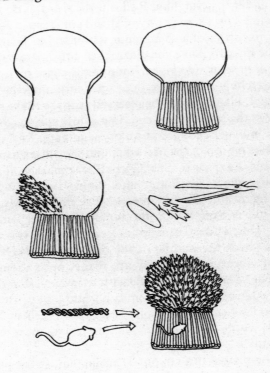

Festival breads

Divide the dough into 2 balls and put 1 to keep soft under the clingfilm. Roll out the other ball to an oblong shape 35 by 24cm (14 by 10in). Cut out a chunky 'button mushroom' shape from the oblong, making the 'stem' about 18cm (7in) long and using the full length and width of the dough. Add the trimmings to the reserved dough and carefully lift the 'mushroom' shape on to the prepared baking sheet. This is your base.

Prick the 'mushroom' shape all over with a fork and brush with water to keep it from drying out. Divide the rest of the dough into a third and two thirds, keeping the two thirds under the clingfilm. Roll out the third of dough to a rectangle 28 by 18cm (11 by 7in) and cut it into 20–30 thin 18cm (7in) strips. These are your wheat stalks. Beat the egg with the milk to make the glaze, then brush some over the 'mushroom stem' and lay all but 6 of the strips on it, side by side, stretching the middle ones up a little into the 'mushroom cap'. Plait or twist the reserved strips to make 2 ties to lay across the stalks at the end. Use a little surplus dough to make a mouse (see illustration on page 127). Lay any surplus stalks on top of the first layer and then glaze them all.

Preheat the oven to 220°C/425°F/gas mark 7. Take the remaining piece of dough and divide it into quarters. Divide again into 24 tiny pieces. Working quickly, shape them between your hands into tapered sausages and, using sharp, pointed scissors, snip into each several times at an angle towards the middle of the dough to make it spiky, like real wheat ears. As they are ready, press them on to the wheat sheaf base, starting with a row overlapping the outside edge of the 'mushroom cap'. Add inner rows, glazing as you go, each overlapping the gaps in the row before, until the whole 'cap' is covered and the ears meet the tops of the stalks.

Lay the plaited ties you made earlier across the junction between stalks and ears.

Glaze again, brushing over the whole finished sheaf. Keep the remaining glaze for the final stage.

Bake the sheaf in the centre of the preheated oven for 15 minutes. Take it out and glaze it once more, then lower the heat to 190°C/375°F/gas mark 5 and bake for another 25–35 minutes, until it is a deep golden brown all over. If you want your sheaf to last for some weeks on display, leave it in the oven after baking, reducing the heat to 120°C/250°F/gas mark ½ for 4 hours or so, until it is thoroughly dry. Cool on a wire rack.

HONEY AND SUNFLOWER SEED BREAD

He should have fed them also with the finest of the
wheat: and with honey out of the rock should I have
satisfied thee.

Psalm 81.16

Allow 2½–3 hours

This is not a traditional festival recipe, but I think it makes
a good bread for any holiday or special occasion as it is
sweetened with honey and enriched with sunflower seeds.

Makes 1 medium loaf

225g/8 oz Granary flour
225g/8 oz strong white flour
1 tsp salt
2 tsp Easyblend dried yeast
2 Tbsp clear honey
275ml/10fl oz warm milk
and water, mixed half
and half
1 Tbsp sunflower oil
75g/3 oz sunflower seeds

> *Cook's tip*
>
> Warm your spoon
> under the hot tap
> before adding the
> honey – it won't
> stick so much

Glaze

1 Tbsp clear honey
2 tsp water
1 Tbsp sunflower seeds

Mix the flours, salt and yeast together in a large bowl.
Make a well in the middle and add the honey, warm milk
and water mixture and oil, stirring to make a soft dough.

Turn it out on to a floured surface and knead for 4–5 minutes, until it is soft and pliable. Return it to the bowl, cover with oiled clingfilm and leave to rise in the warm for 1–1½ hours, until it has doubled in size. Grease a baking sheet.

Knock down the dough on a floured surface and gradually mix in the sunflower seeds, folding the dough and kneading them in.

Shape the dough into a round cob and place it on the prepared baking sheet to prove. Cover it with oiled clingfilm or upturn the mixing bowl over it and leave in a warm place for 30–40 minutes.

Preheat the oven to 200°C/400°F/gas mark 6.

When the dough has risen well again, remove the clingfilm or bowl. Now make the glaze. Warm the honey and water together in a small saucepan and glaze the loaf. Scatter with sunflower seeds and bake in the centre of the preheated oven for 25–30 minutes.

Cool on a rack.

5

Recipes using bread as a main ingredient

Any food eaten daily will sometimes be left over, so this chapter aims to give you some ideas as to how to use up leftover bread.

Breadcrumbs

One obvious solution is to make breadcrumbs, which can then be frozen in small containers until needed. An electric liquidiser is the easiest way to make fresh breadcrumbs.

USING LEFTOVER BREAD: THE MIDDLE AGES

Break the bread into smallish pieces, switch on the machine and drop the bread through the hole in the lid on to the twirling blades. Do a few at a time.

To make dry breadcrumbs, put pieces of stale bread in a low oven to dry out completely. Then, put in a polythene bag, seal and crush with a rolling pin. Be careful not to overcrush them into dust. These can be kept in an airtight tin or plastic box.

Melba Toast

Melba toast (or 'scrunch' as my grandmother called it) is a very good way to use up stale white bread.

Slice the bread as thinly as you easily can and toast each side. Then, lay each piece down and cut the toast horizontally with a sharp serrated knife to make two even thinner slices. Lay these, soft side up, on a baking sheet and bake in a 180°C/350°F/gas mark 4 oven until they are golden brown and crisp – about 10 minutes, but keep an eye on them as they will burn if you look away. Cool on a wire rack and store, when cold, in an airtight tin. They are delicious with pâtés, cheese or any other favourite topping and will keep for months.

Croûtons

These are a delicious addition to soups or salads. They are small cubes of bread (white or brown, crusts removed) either baked in the oven or fried in butter or oil. One way is to put the cubes in a bowl, moisten them with olive oil, flavour with crushed thyme and garlic and, when the cubes are well impregnated, spread them on a baking sheet and bake them at 180°C/350°F/gas mark 4 for 10 minutes or so, until lightly golden and crisp. Be careful not to let them burn. Once made, you can keep them warm in a very low oven or let them cool and reheat them when needed.

Garlic Bread

Allow 25 minutes

Even a day-old baguette can be improved by this treatment.

Soften 100g (3½ oz) butter on a plate. Crush 1–2 cloves of garlic into the butter. Make deep slashes in the baguette, cutting more than halfway through. Spread the inside of each cut with the garlic butter and smear any remaining butter over the loaf with your hand. Wrap the whole loaf in foil and bake in a moderate oven for 15–20 minutes. Serve hot, and let each guest tear off a slice or two.

Bruschetta

Tuscany's version of garlic bread.

Toast slices of rough country bread on both sides – preferably over a wood fire, but otherwise under the grill. Rub a crushed half clove of garlic all over one side of the hot toast, leaving shreds of garlic on the bread, and repeat with more garlic on the other slices, or give each person their slice and half a garlic clove to rub in themselves. Sprinkle with salt and pepper, moisten liberally with olive oil and eat straight away with a glass of robust red wine.

This is the basic bruschetta, but you can embellish it by covering the garlic with chopped ripe tomatoes, raw onion or anchovy fillets, or hand round a selection and let your guests make up their own combinations. Don't skimp on the oil.

Crostini

A more sophisticated appetiser than bruschetta, crostini are slices of French bread, sometimes untoasted but more often toasted or baked and then spread with a tasty pâté or some chopped egg, tomato or mushroom. Here are recipes for two favourite spreads for crostini.

Chicken Liver Pâté

Serves 4–6

250g/8 oz chicken livers
2 Tbsp olive oil
50g/2 oz butter
1 garlic clove, crushed
4 Tbsp marsala or sweet sherry
sprig of fresh thyme, leaves pulled off

Fry the chicken livers gently in the oil and butter with the garlic for 4–5 minutes – they should still be pink inside. Add the marsala or sherry and thyme leaves and remove from the heat. Mash together in a mortar or blend to a paste in a liquidiser or food processor. Spread on crostini or hot toast and serve. This pâté keeps well in the fridge – simply melt a little butter and pour over the top to seal.

Tapenade (Olive Paste)

Serves 4–6

150g/5 oz black olives, stoned
4 anchovies, chopped
2 Tbsp capers, drained
1–2 garlic cloves, crushed
5 Tbsp olive oil

Blend all the ingredients briefly in a food processor – chop them finely rather than reduce them to a liquid. Alternatively chop them on a board with a mezzaluna or sharp knife until they coalesce enough to spread on hot toast. It will keep well in an airtight container in the fridge.

TARAMASALATA

Allow 20–30 minutes

This delicious Greek smoked fish pâté is traditionally made with grey mullet roe – botargo – but smoked cod's roe makes a good substitute, though it can be hard to find. Slices of stale, crustless white bread are softened in water, then squeezed out and added to reduce the saltiness of the fish and bulk out the pâté.

Serves 4–6

 250g/8 oz smoked cod's roe
 2 slices of white bread, medium/thick, crusts removed
 1–2 garlic cloves, crushed
 juice of 1 lemon
 200–250ml/6–8fl oz olive oil or olive and groundnut oil
  mixed
 black olives, to garnish
 toast to serve

Remove the skin from the roe if necessary. Soak the bread in a little water, then squeeze dry. Either pound the roe in a mortar or round bowl with a pestle or strong wooden spoon or whizz it in a food processor. Add 1 of the cloves of garlic and continue to mash or pulse, adding the lemon juice, oil and bread gradually to make a thick, smooth paste. Taste and judge if you need to add more oil, lemon juice or garlic. Serve garnished with black olives on hot toast.

LOCKET'S SAVOURY

Allow 20–30 minutes

The contrast between sweet pears, salty blue cheese and peppery watercress makes this savoury particularly good. It is named after the restaurant in London where it was invented.

Serves 4

- 8 small slices white bread or 4 large, halved
- 1 large bunch of watercress
- 4 ripe pears, well flavoured – a good Comice, perhaps – peeled and thinly sliced
- 350g/12 oz Stilton cheese, thinly sliced
- freshly ground black pepper

Preheat the oven to 180°C/350°F/gas mark 4.

Toast the bread and remove the crusts. Lay the toast on a baking sheet and, first, arrange the watercress over the top, then the slices of pear. Cover with the slices of Stilton.

Bake in the preheated oven for 10 minutes, or until the cheese begins to melt. Grind black pepper over before serving. These are very good but quite messy to eat in the hand – better on a plate with a knife and fork.

PAPPA AL POMODORO AND PANZANELLA

Perhaps it is because the flat, saltless loaves of Pane Basso (see page 71), so delicious when fresh, are much less appetising a day or two later, that the Tuscans have devised so many ways of using up stale loaves. Bread is routinely added to soups, stews and salads as a thickener. It is also a good vehicle for strong flavours.

Tomatoes, ripe and juicy, go particularly well with stale bread – here are two recipes to prove it. First, a substantial tomato soup – Pappa al Pomodoro – and, second, a tomato and bread salad called Panzanella.

PAPPA AL POMODORO

Allow 30–40 minutes

Serves 6

1kg/2lbs large, ripe tomatoes
300g/10 oz stale country bread (white or brown or mixed)
a small onion, chopped
4 cloves of garlic, finely chopped
6 Tbsp best olive oil, plus more for serving
few sprigs fresh basil and sage
salt and freshly ground black pepper, to taste
2 litres/3 pints light chicken stock (made using 1 stock cube)

Put the tomatoes in a bowl, cover with boiling water, leave for a few minutes and then slip the skins off. Cut them up small. Shave any very hard crusts off the bread and slice finely.

Soften the onion and garlic in the olive oil in a large

pan, add the chopped tomatoes and basil and sage. Season to taste with salt and pepper. Gradually add the chicken stock to the pan and put in the pieces of bread as you add the stock, until all are in. Bring to the boil, then simmer, so that the bread swells and absorbs most of the liquid, making a pap, or, 'pappa' in Italian. Leave to settle, check the seasoning and then serve in hot bowls with a drizzle of oil over each.

PANZANELLA

Allow 45 minutes

This recipe, for a tomato and bread salad, is really like a Tuscan version of gazpacho – that wonderful chilled Spanish soup, but, for the Tuscans, the bread is a more important ingredient so there is less liquid. Use the best-quality bread, tomatoes and oil that you can find.

'A loaf of bread', the Walrus said,
'is what we chiefly need.
Pepper and vinegar besides
Are very good indeed.'

Lewis Carroll, *Alice through the Looking Glass*

Serves 6

   200g/7 oz good coarse white bread, a day old, crusts
      removed
   6 large, ripe tomatoes, chopped or roughly sliced
   1 red onion, finely sliced
   ½ cucumber, finely sliced
   2 celery sticks, finely sliced
   handful of fresh basil

6 Tbsp olive oil
2 Tbsp wine vinegar
salt and freshly ground black pepper, to taste

Slice the bread thickly and cut it into small pieces. Put it into a salad bowl and sprinkle with cold water – enough so that it is well moistened, but not soggy (if your hand slips, squeeze out the surplus water). Add the chopped or sliced vegetables, tear the basil into strips and dress it all with the oil and vinegar and season to taste. Stir it gently and then leave for half an hour or more for the bread to absorb the dressing. Serve chilled.

BREAD SAUCE

Allow ½ hour, but best made some hours before using

Most of us still eat bread sauce at Christmas with the turkey, if not more often. Made with good-quality bread, rich milk and seasoned with pungent mace, it is a very good accompaniment to the roast bird. Mace is the outer husk of the nutmeg and is bought as a separate spice.

Serves 6–8

    1 small onion, stuck with 4 cloves
    ½ litre/¾ pint full-cream milk
    100g/3–4 oz day-old breadcrumbs
    ½–1 tsp mace or nutmeg, ground
    salt and freshly ground black pepper to taste
    1–2 pinches cayenne pepper
    1 Tbsp butter or 2 Tbsp double cream

Put the onion and milk in a double boiler (or a bowl set over simmering water) and let it heat through gradually until it is nearly boiling and the flavours of the onion and cloves have infused the milk. Remove the onion, which will have softened a little and, discarding the cloves, chop the onion finely and return it to the hot milk.

Continue using the double boiler or basin over the hot water and whisk in the breadcrumbs until the sauce is thick and the milk has been absorbed, adding more crumbs or milk as needed. Season with the mace or nutmeg, salt and black and cayenne peppers. It can now keep warm for several hours without harm, off the direct heat.

Before serving, stir in the butter or cream and pour into a sauceboat or tureen.

PIZZA NAPOLETANA

Allow 3 hours – 1½ hours for the dough + 45 minutes for the tomato sauce + 45 minutes for laying and baking

Using leftover dough rather than stale bread, the pizza has evolved all over the Mediterranean and remains a delicious snack or meal. You can still buy slices of pizza from large rectangular tins in Italian bakeries.

Use 450g (1lb) dough left over from one of the basic white breads in Chapter 1 or else make the dough from scratch, as given below, which means that you can enrich it with egg, milk or olive oil if you like and achieve a lighter, more nourishing pizza.

The Neapolitan version of pizza is simple, classic and delicious. The mozzarella is optional – ask your consumers if they want it on their section.

Makes 1 large pizza

Dough

   450g/1lb strong white flour
   2 tsp salt
   15g/½ oz fresh yeast or 2 tsp Easyblend dried yeast
   150ml/¼ pint milk, warmed
   1 large egg
   100ml/3–4fl oz olive oil

Tomato sauce

   1kg/2lbs tomatoes, fresh and skinned if in season or
      tinned or a mixture
   2 medium onions, finely chopped
   2 Tbsp olive oil

3 garlic cloves, crushed
salt and freshly ground black pepper
dried or fresh oregano, to taste
pinch of sugar

Topping

tin anchovy fillets
15–20 black olives, stoned and chopped
1 ball mozzarella cheese (optional)
olive oil, to drizzle
dried or fresh oregano, to sprinkle

Mix the flour and salt and Easyblend dried yeast, if using, in a large bowl and stand in the warm. If using the fresh yeast, stir it into the warm milk in a small bowl, melting it into a cream. Make a well in the centre of the flour and pour in the milk, break in the egg and add 4 tablespoons of the oil. Mix to a dough with your hand, adding more oil until you have a smooth, elastic dough that comes cleanly away from the bowl. Cover with a damp cloth or oiled clingfilm and set in a warm place to rise until doubled in size, 1–1½ hours.

Meanwhile make the tomato sauce.

Chop the skinned or tinned tomatoes roughly. Soften the onions in the oil in a large frying pan without browning. Add the garlic, then the tomatoes and let it all bubble together over a higher heat to let the water evaporate, stirring from time to time.

Season with salt (not too much as there are olives and anchovies to come), pepper, the oregano and sugar and continue to cook until the sauce has thickened nicely.

Take a rectangular baking sheet with a shallow rim and brush it with olive oil.

When the dough has risen, knock back on a floured

board, flouring your hands to prevent sticking, and place it in the middle of the prepared baking sheet. Spread it out to cover the tin, pressing with your knuckles to encourage it outwards. If it keeps shrinking back, let it rest for a few minutes and then try again. Preheat the oven to 230°C/450°F/gas mark 8.

Spread the tomato sauce over the dough, then add the topping. Scatter with torn pieces of anchovy fillets and black olives and small pieces of mozzarella, if using it. Drizzle olive oil over it all, sprinkle the oregano over and leave in a warm place for a few minutes to let the dough recover and begin rising again.

Bake in the preheated oven for 20–25 minutes, beginning on the centre shelf, then moving the pizza to a lower shelf after 15 minutes. If you have an Aga, use the bottom of the hot oven for the final 10 minutes.

Serve hot, with fruity red wine.

Recipes using bread as a main ingredient

FRENCH TOAST
(PAIN PERDU OR EGGY BREAD)

Allow 5–10 minutes

A delicious, nourishing way to use up stale white bread and an instant pudding to make while the family sits around the kitchen table.

You need bread, milk, eggs, butter, sugar and a frying pan.

Soften each slice, or half slice, of stale bread in milk. Dip it in egg beaten with a little sugar, then fry it lightly in butter, turning when it is golden and crisp on one side to cook the other. Dust with caster sugar and serve immediately.

You can keep it savoury by omitting the sugar and serving it with ketchup.

For a sweet variation, try mixing a little cinnamon with the sugar. For a grander version, use slices of stale brioche and milk flavoured with a vanilla pod and sugar. As always, the quality of the bread you use determines the taste of the final dish.

APRICOT OR PLUM TOASTS

Allow 45 minutes

Another quick, nourishing pudding for family consumption.

You need day-old white bread, butter, sugar and fruit.

Butter some slices of stale white bread and put them on a buttered baking sheet. Stone the apricots or plums, halve them and lay them – cut side up – on the bread, three or four to a slice. Fill the hollows left by the stones with sugar and press the fruit down on the bread.

Bake in a 180°C/350°F/gas mark 4 oven for 30 minutes or so, until the bread is crisp and the fruit soft and sticky. Serve hot.

BREAD AND BUTTER PUDDING

Allow 5 hours (3 hours for soaking the fruit + 2 hours for making and baking)

One of those nursery puddings that remains a favourite into adulthood. The rum is an adult addition. You can make it even richer by using cream and milk instead of just milk. In any case, use full-cream milk, plenty of butter and good-quality bread. The standing time is important as this allows the bread to swell.

Serves 4–6

- 50g/2 oz sultanas or currants
- 25g/1 oz candied peel, chopped
- 3 Tbsp rum
- 3 eggs
- 450ml/¾ pint full-cream milk or 300ml/½ pint milk and 150ml/¼ pint single cream
- 6 large or 9 medium slices of white bread, crusts removed, thickly buttered and cut into wide fingers
- 50g/2 oz demerara sugar

Soak the sultanas and peel in the rum overnight or for 3–4 hours.

Break the eggs into a large bowl and beat them with a whisk. Heat the milk or milk and cream to just below boiling, remove from the heat and gradually whisk into the eggs. Strain the soaked fruit from the rum and set aside. Add the rum to the egg and milk mixture.

Grease a large pie dish or rectangular ovenproof dish with butter and use one third of the bread to line the bottom. Spread over half the soaked fruit. Repeat both layers and finish with the third layer of bread on top, butter-side up, overlapping the slices to make a nice texture.

Sprinkle with half the sugar, pour the egg and milk mixture over and leave to stand for 30 minutes or so. Meanwhile, preheat the oven to 150°C/300°F/gas mark 2.

Finally, sprinkle the remaining sugar over and bake in the oven for 45–60 minutes, until the custard has set and the top is crusty.

Variation

Chocolate Bread and Butter Pudding
Melt a 100-g (3½-oz) bar of dark chocolate in 2 tablespoons of the milk or milk and cream and add to the custard mixture before the rum.

DELIA SMITH'S CHUNKY MARMALADE BREAD AND BUTTER PUDDING

Another delicious variation on the bread and butter pudding theme, for which we are grateful to Delia Smith.

Serves 4–6

  6 slices white bread, from a good-quality large loaf,
      1cm/½in thick with crusts left on
  50g/2 oz softened butter
  2 rounded Tbsp Seville orange marmalade
  275ml/10fl oz full-cream milk
  60ml/2½fl oz double cream
  3 large eggs
  75g/3 oz sugar
  grated zest of 1 large orange
  1 Tbsp demerara sugar
  25g/1 oz candied peel, finely chopped

To serve

  Crème fraîche or chilled pouring cream

Preheat the oven to 180°C/350°F/gas mark 4.

First, generously butter the slices of bread on one side, then spread the marmalade on 3 of these slices, and put the other 3 slices on top (buttered-side down) so you've got 3 rounds of sandwiches. Now spread some butter over the top slice of each sandwich and cut each one into quarters to make little triangles or squares.

Then arrange the sandwiches, butter-side up, overlapping each other in a lightly buttered baking dish 18 by 23cm (7 by 9in) and 5cm (2in) deep and standing almost upright. After that, whisk the milk, cream, eggs and sugar together and pour this all over the bread. Scatter the surface of the bread with the grated orange zest, demerara sugar and candied peel, then place the pudding on a high shelf and bake it for 35–40 minutes until it's puffy and golden and the top crust is crunchy.

Serve the pudding straight from the oven while it's still puffy, with either crème fraîche or chilled pouring cream.

Recipes using bread as a main ingredient

BROWN BETTY

Allow 1½ hours

This is a homely version of Apple Charlotte, a lovely pudding for autumn, when there are lots of windfall apples about, though other fruit in their seasons, such as gooseberries, plums or apricots, work perfectly well, too. It is a very good use for stale white bread – the better the quality of the bread, the better the pudding. The quantities given in the recipe will feed 4–6 people, but you can easily diminish or augment them to adjust the size of the pudding to suit.

Serves 4–6

    6–8 slices (depending on the size of the loaf) good-
        quality stale white bread
    60–90g/2–3 oz butter, softened
    c. 1kg/2lbs apples, peeled, cored and thinly sliced,
        cookers or eaters or a mixture
    6 Tbsp demerara sugar or golden syrup
    zest and juice of 1 small lemon
    1 tsp ground cinnamon
    cream or custard to serve

Preheat the oven to 180°C/350°F/gas mark 4 and butter a round 1.5-litre (2½-pint) capacity heatproof dish.

Thickly butter the slices of bread and cut each slice into quarters (leave the crust on unless it is very tough). Using a third of the slices, put a layer of bread over the bottom of the prepared dish, butter side up, and then lay half the apple slices over it. Mix the sugar or golden syrup with the grated lemon zest and the cinnamon and sprinkle 2 tablespoons of it over the fruit. Repeat the layering with bread and then the rest of the fruit. Sprinkle it with another

153

2 tablespoons of the sugar mixture and the juice of the lemon.

Finally, arrange the rest of the bread on top, overlapping the slices to cover the whole surface. Scatter the rest of the sugar, or syrup mixture over and bake in the preheated oven for 40–50 minutes, until the apples are cooked and the top is golden brown and crusty. Serve with cream or custard.

Recipes using bread as a main ingredient

BREAD PUDDING

Allow 2½ hours

One used to see dark rectangular slabs of bread pudding, heavy with dried fruit, in most bakers' shops, sold either by the slice or by weight. They were, and are, a very good way of using up stale bread, however hard and board-like it may be. It is very quick to mix, though needs a long time in the oven. It is perfect for lunchboxes or eaten hot as a pudding, with custard, of course.

This version is from *Warne's Model Cookery and Housekeeping Book*, published in 1868. You can vary the fruit, the spices, add marmalade or fresh grated apple or whatever you like – it's an accommodating recipe.

Makes 1 large loaf

- c. 240g/8 oz stale bread, white or brown – preferably a variety – crust and crumb
- c. 300ml/½ pint hot milk or water
- 90g/3 oz soft dark sugar
- c. 240g/8 oz mixed dried fruit – raisins, currants, sultanas and candied peel if you like
- grated zest of 1 lemon
- freshly grated nutmeg
- 2 eggs, beaten

Preheat the oven to 165°C/325°F/gas mark 3 and grease a 1.25-litre/2-lb loaf tin, lining the bottom with baking parchment.

Break the stale bread up into smallish pieces and put them into a medium-sized bowl. Cover with the hot milk or water and leave to soften for a few minutes. Beat them smooth with a fork, stir in the sugar, dried fruit and lemon zest and grate in a little nutmeg. Finally, beat in the eggs and pour the mixture into your greased and lined loaf tin.

Bake in the preheated oven for 1½ hours, then increase the heat to 180°C/350°F/gas mark 4 for another half an hour. Leave it to cool in the tin. It will be heavy, moist and delicious.

QUEEN OF PUDDINGS

Allow 1½ hours

Known as Queen's Pudding when I was small and a regular choice for birthday meals. The Orange Pudding variation is well worth trying and rather less sweet.

Serves 4–6

150g/6 oz fresh white breadcrumbs
125g/4 oz caster sugar
grated zest of 1 lemon
600ml/1 pint full-cream milk
50g/2 oz butter
3 eggs, separated
3–4 Tbsp raspberry or strawberry jam

Preheat the oven to 180°C/350°F/gas mark 4. Put the breadcrumbs, 1 heaped tablespoon of the sugar and the lemon zest into a large bowl. Heat the milk with the butter in a pan, bring nearly to the boil, then pour over the breadcrumb mixture and leave to cool for 10–15 minutes.

Beat in the egg yolks and pour it all into a 1.2-litre (2-pint) ovenproof dish and bake in the preheated oven for about 30 minutes, until the top has just set. Remove from the oven and lower the temperature to 150°C/300°F/gas mark 2.

Spread the jam over the surface of the custardy mixture in the dish. Whisk the egg whites until stiff, add half the remaining sugar and whisk again. Fold in the rest of the sugar with a metal spoon and cover the jam with meringue, spooning it up into billowy shapes. Return the pudding to the oven for 15–20 minutes, to let the meringue cook gently and take colour. Serve hot.

Variation

Orange Pudding
Use brown breadcrumbs instead of white, orange zest instead of lemon zest and a bitter marmalade (not too chunky) instead of the jam. You can also slice the flesh of the orange finely (removing any pith) and lay the slices over the marmalade before topping with the meringue.

Go thy way, eat thy bread with joy, and drink thy wine with a merry heart.

Ecclesiastes 9.7

Select Bibliography

Recommended for further reference and reading for pleasure:

David, Elizabeth (1977) *English Bread and Yeast Cooking*, Allan & Lane.

Grant, Doris (1944) *Your Daily Bread*, Faber & Faber.

Ingram, Christine, and Shapter, Jennie (2000) *The World Encyclopaedia of Bread and Bread-making*, Anness Publishing.

Jaine, Tom (1995) *Making Bread at Home*, Weidenfeld & Nicholson.

Scurfield, George and Cecilia (1956) *Home Baked*, Faber & Faber.

Walker, Lorna, and Hughes, Joyce (1977) *The Complete Bread Book*, Hamlyn.

Index